MYTHWAKERS

MYTHWAKERS

THE MINOTAUR

KATE RISTAU

Copyright © 2023 by Hope Well Books

Cover design: Gigi Little

Interior design: Kate Ristau

First Edition, June 2023

Printed in the United States of America

ISBN: 978-1-7370879-4-6

I. Mythology, Greek—Juvenile Literature. 2. Gods, Greek—Juvenile
Literature.

JUVENILE NONFICTION / Social Science / Folklore & Mythology,
JNF052030

This book uses Meridian Font.

For bulk orders, please contact orders@hopewellbooks.com.

The series was made possible by a grant from the Regional Arts and
Culture Council and from Kickstarter backers. Keep supporting the
arts, my friends! Make the world a better place.

To Mom, for inspiring my love of Greek mythology;
to Rowan, for asking for another story;
to the University of Oregon Folklore Department,
for showing me the myth,
and to Bob, for helping make the magic.

CONTENTS

THE MINOTAUR

Hi! My name is Asterion! I am a Minotaur. You may recognize me from such books as *Clockbreakers* by Kate Ristau, or from old-timey poems and epic stories written by guys like Ovid and Plutarch. Those authors got some things right, but they got more than a few things wrong, and I'm here to set the historical record straight.

My life is pretty a-maze-ing. Get it?

That joke never gets old, even after all these years. I mean, you could almost get lost in it.

Like a maze.

Moving on, I am so glad you are here. I am a Myth-waker — a legendary character from an ancient myth that has come to define an entire generation. What? You

1. You are going to see lots of awesome photos of me in Mythwakers. Each one of these photos has a number so you can find more information in the back of the book under sources.

don't know what a myth is? Dude. You're going to love this. Pull up a chair, get comfortable, and we'll explore myths, mazes, and most importantly: me.

Myths

A lot of people use myth to mean a fake story. That's one meaning of the word myth, but the kind of myths I am talking about are **mythology** — the foundational narratives, or stories, of a particular culture.

Sorry. I used a lot of big words there. All those centuries trapped in the **labyrinth** (that endless maze) were SUPER BORING, so I read a lot of scrolls.

Back to **myths** — just think of them as the important beginning stories of a group of people.

The group of people — or **culture** — that we will be talking about today is the Greeks, and a little bit about those Minoan dudes, too.

Here's an important thing for you to know: people argue a lot about my story. Some people think it happened. Other people think it didn't. Some people think Theseus is a hero, while smart people know that he is a ding-dong.

That's the thing about myths — they are around for a long time, passed down from one person to the next, so not all the versions are the same. Think about if your best friend told you a story, which you turned around and told your grandma. Would you tell the same exact story your friend told you to your kind, gentle grandmother? Would you keep all the bloody parts or would you clean things up a bit? You would probably make a few changes, right?

Most of us do, and that is why myths are never told the same way twice.

Best friend story, now featuring:

- Blood and guts!
- Nasty villains!
- Mean kids!
- Burps and farts!
- Tacos!

Grandma story, politely exploring:

- Talking animals.
- Snuggly kittens.
- Flowers and smiles.
- Five guys named Alfred.
- Hard candy.

Stories change depending on who is telling them and who is listening to them. If you're talking to your best friend, you might be shouting about fiery salsa and guacamole. If you are sweetly sitting beside your grandma, you could be whispering about butterscotch and rainbows.

That's the thing about myths: the audience matters.

How we remember myths has a lot to do with who was telling the story and who was listening. The stories were constantly changing, but the ones that hung around were the ones that people remembered. They appealed to the culture. They mattered to the listeners. In this way, the audience and the storytellers can change myths for the good, for the bad, and for the tacos.

Folklore

Tacos are good, but they aren't folklore. **Folklore** is the stories, art, and culture we create and pass down to one another.

Sometimes, we write our stories in books — like this one! Other times, we share our stories in plays or over dinner. Sometimes we text stories to our friends, or flood them with a never-ending stream of emojis. Folklore is a word we can use to explain all those artistic things we share that are so important, well, we do them over and over again.

Myths are folklore, too — they are stories that have been told and retold again and again. They are shared because they are stories that matter to us and to our community.

All right. That's enough from me. You think you already know what folklore is, so it is time for a super easy test! Ace it, and you'll be a legend too.

Circle the examples of folklore below

Tacos - Riddles - Folk art
Rhyming games - Fairy tales - Mustard
Jokes - A license plate - 2+3
Street art - Folk music - Your phone number

Tacos, Mustard, A license plate, 2+3, and Your phone number are not folklore, but folk music definitely is, and so are all those fairy tales your mom told you. Everything else on that list above is also folklore — artistic things that we do and share with each other a lot.

What about you? What are some things that you create and share with your family and friends? Do you tell stories? Make memes? Sing songs? Tell jokes? Draw comics? What do you love to do?

Things I love to create and share

1

2

3

4

5

If you said design punk rock posters, high five! If you said paint pet rocks, high hoof! You rock, and clearly, you make and participate in folklore all the time.

Folklore matters

A myth is a kind of folklore, too, but not everything is folklore. For something to become folklore, it has to really matter to us. The things that last — the things that stick around and that we want to share over and over again with our family and friends — there's a reason they have that staying power. It's because they show who we are and what is important to us.

For example, I really like hoof rubs, but did that make it into my myth? No! That's because me getting awesome hoof rubs didn't matter as much to the people telling my story: the Greeks.

Enough about folklore! Let's talk about me.

The Man, the Monster, the Myth

2. *William Blake, a poet and printmaker, made me look super intimidating in this illustration. He understood the assignment.*

Now, some people say I have the body of a man and the head of a bull. Others say I am half-cow and half-man. I say they are half-rude and I am one-hundred-and-eighty-nine-percent awesome.

I was born this way, with spectacular horns, furry ears, and muscles for days. I also have a nice long tail like any decent Minotaur.

I know. This is where the arguments begin. Some people think I have brown eyes. Some people think they are blue. Some people think smokes pours out of my nostrils — I wish! That would be epic. Except when I was blowing my nose. I would keep lighting all the tissues on fire.

Achoo! AHHHHH!!!

It's a good thing I don't have a fire-nose. Or feet. Can you imagine? Some people think I have human feet — like toes and stuff. This is SO TOTALLY NOT TRUE. I don't have feet! I have hooves — long, sharp, glorious hooves.

Honestly, if the stories had included nice, long hoof rubs, we wouldn't be having this discussion, would we?

3. Here I am in an engraving by Paul Gustave Louis Christophe Doré. Are those toes? Ewww. Gross.

Ah, well. Not very many people survived the labyrinth (super not my fault), so they don't really know what I look like, I guess.

What? No! I don't look like a horse! Neigh, I don't! Why would you say that? Fine, maybe, when you see super-old drawings of me, sometimes I maybe look just a very tiny bit like a possible horse, but clearly, I am not a horse. I am part bovine, not equine.

4. I am not a horse in this photograph of a shallow bowl with an illustration of Theseus poking me. Super impolite, Theseus.

Sorry, touchy subject. You see, those paintings make me look like I'm a horse because those people don't know how to draw a bull.

As a side note, if you ever see a statue of me without

any hands, that's because it's an old statue and the hands broke off. I have awesome hands. Amazing hands. Unbelievable hands. Monstrous hands!

5. This statue used to be on a fountain. It also used to have hands.

On the other hand (ha!), while I am the Minotaur from all the stories, it's rude to call someone by what they are, as opposed to their name. I mean, I don't go around calling you a scrawny human, do I?

Should I?

No? Okay. Then, you can call me by my real name, which is Asterion, as opposed to Manly Minotaur, Bull Guy, or That Cow Man over there.

Asterion means starry. You can find **constellations**, or groups of stars, that tell my story. Look up into the sky for the Corona Borealis, or the northern crown. It is the crown of my sister, Ariadne. Every time I look up, I am reminded of her long golden hair. She shines so bright.

You don't need to get out your telescope, though, and be all space-y. I'll stick around and tell you lots more about me, including why they keep retelling my story, from Hollywood to the heavens and beyond.

THE SETTING

Now, when someone sits down to tell you a story, they usually begin with the **setting** — the time and place of the story. Some stories take place in forests, while others are set in schools or on playgrounds. I have even read a story that took place in an intergalactic, cosmic restroom (you should hear the sound of those interstellar flushes).

There weren't that many fancy toilets back in the time of my story. In fact, most of us didn't even have running water, more or less automatic hand dryers. Seriously, we are talking super ancient history, way back before your mom was alive and even before the time of your Great Aunt Melda. Several **millennia** - thousands of years.

Both time and place matter to the setting when you are telling a story, so we are going to dive into both.

The thing is, while you might think my story takes place in Ancient Greece, that's not exactly true.

Crete

My life, and my story, began on an island called **Crete** (Kreet), in the city of **Knossos** (like Nah, sis). Let me show you around the wonderful island that I call my home.

6. The beautiful island of Crete — my Mediterranean home.

Crete is a large island in the Mediterranean Sea, just off the coast of Greece. It's sunny and warm in the north most of the year, and a little bit cooler in the south. If you're planning a visit, stop by, say hi, and I'll be your tour guide! Make sure you come sometime between July through September, when the ocean is warm and the **Loukoumades** (Loo-koo-ma-daze) are hot. What? You've never had loukoumades? Now you have to come visit. It's the most delicious fried dough covered in ice cream, nuts, and a drizzle of honey.

I always order my loukoumades with extra honey, so they are sweet as ambrosia on a summer afternoon. Let's practice out loud so you're ready to place your order.

Say it loud and proud aloud with me: Loo-koo-MA-daze. Loo-koo-MA-daze. Loo-koo-MA-daze. Loo-koo-

MA-daze! Nicely done. Order up! Sink your teeth into those delicious delicacies.

From the Mountains to the Sea

Once you're done eating, there are mountains to climb, oceans to swim, and even a desert to explore (though I would prefer to explore dessert again).

7. A journey to my island home takes you over high mountains and back down again to the sea.

Pack your bag, and let's start our journey! You're going to love Crete. While the island is 160 miles long, it's only about seven and a half miles wide. That means if you brought a good pair of sandals, you could easily walk from one side to the other in a day.

Well, you'd have to be in *really* good shape to hike from Knossos to Gortyna (Vort-een-a). There will be more than a few mountains in your way. Crete is a mountainous island, including three main mountain ranges:

1. The Idi Range
2. The White Mountains
3. The Dikti Mountains

Which mountain range would you like to climb? Circle which one, gather your gear, and draw a picture of a mountain next to the list above. Soon, you'll be off on your next big adventure!

Sea to Shinier Sea

But as you pack for the mountains, don't forget your swimsuit. Crete is known for its sandy beaches and rocky shores. In fact, you can sun your hooves on pink sand beaches. The sand crystals shine in the morning sun. Spend a day in the warm lagoon of Elafonisi (Hey-la-phone-ee-see) Beach before you pack up for Mount Pachnes in the White Mountains. Pachnes is a desert mountain with a barren landscape. It will be your first mountain trek as you head across Crete.

Highlanders know their way around the mountains in Crete. But if you are a lowlander, and you miss one of the well-worn paths through the valleys, you could end up on top of a plateau, having to hike miles out of your way to get to the other beach. It is always a good idea to carry a map in Crete. I am going to share a few maps in the back of the book if you want to know more about my wonderful island home. Just check out the **Find Out More** section.

The Minoans

My culture (my group of peeps) is not the Greeks, even though my story is in every Greek Mythology book you will ever read. I am just that a-maze-ing. In reality, though, I'm not Greek (they're the audience for my story, remember?). I am from the **Minoan** Culture.

Wait a minute...Minoan? Does that sound familiar to you? Yes! That's right! I'm the mino-taur.

Minotaur means "the bull of Minos" in Ancient Greek. Minos was the King of Crete (nasty dude. We'll talk about him later). I can't believe I was named after him. Really, you should call me Asterion. That's way more polite than naming me after the guy that trapped me in that infinitely boring, interminably endless, utterly unending labyrinth.

More about him later. Or not. It's my story, and just thinking about him is making me grumpy.

Time for some more Loo-koo-MA-daze! Honey. Nuts. Delicious ice cream. Maybe even a sprinkle of cinnamon to spice things up a bit. Yum. I'm feeling better already.

Fragments in time

You know, I'm an old dude. Not as old as Zeus, but the original Asteria, the starry Titaness that I was named after, gave birth to Hecate, the goddess of witchcraft and magic (or maybe she didn't). Asteria's father was either

Perses or Zeus (or maybe they weren't). Historians are still trying to figure that one out, just like they are debating my story (always arguing!). When stories are around so long, there tend to be a few disagreements along the way (totally!). Luckily, we have real, physical evidence to help figure out the story of what happened to me (and we can stop with the parentheses).

Archaeologists have been digging up and searching for evidence of ancient civilizations like mine — the Minoan Civilization — for hundreds of years. In the 21st Century, they use their shovels, brushes and spades to uncover the stories of who we are and what happened to us. In this way, the past is not forgotten. It is just another story waiting to be told.

Evidence

The first evidence you can find of me is around the seventh century BCE — that's negative 700. Around that time, the Chinese had just invented printing. Since the Internet wasn't available back then, archaeologists nowadays search beneath the rocks and ruins of Crete. They look for the everyday tools and items we used so they can understand our story. They dig though the rubble and remains of our towns and cities to find out who we were and what mattered to us.

Modern understanding about the Minoans is based on fragments and pieces. Archaeologists are still trying to understand the larger picture. They have found lots of **amphoras** — fancy, decorated storage containers. If I had one, I'd fill mine with Loo-koo-MA-daze. Anyways, one amphora shows Theseus and I...having a really good conversation about swords.

8. An amphora that was hopefully filled with Loukoumades.

The Greeks liked to decorate their pottery with images and stories that mattered to them, like stories about me (and that loser Theseus).

While the first evidence of me doesn't show up until those old pots, my story takes place long before that pottery was thrown (not thrown across the room! They say pottery is thrown when you are making it. Stop it! Don't throw your hot cocoa mug at me!).

You see, the culture of Crete was exploding (in a good way) around 1600 BCE. Archaeologists have uncovered multi-story palaces, built of stone, from that time period. They were majestic. Remember what I was saying about intergalactic toilets? Well, the queen even had a flushing toilet. Seriously! Crete was the epitome of civilization at the time. They weren't just building fancy bathrooms. In fact, Crete is Europe's most ancient civilization. They were number one. Not number two. Ha! Sorry, I'll stop being such a potty mouth.

From Pottery to Poetry

While we don't have written stories from that time, later on, the great Greek poet Homer spoke of the Cretan city of Gortyna in his famous poem, *The Odyssey*. I remember how the words rolled off his tongue. Sit back, relax, and enjoy my retelling of that story:

> At the end of the Trojan War,
> Our heroes were blown off course,
> Beyond the stormy seas and more,
> They crashed into Gortnya's shore.
> How unfair! How dumb!
> Something, something, Loo-koo-MA-daze!

Listen, we can't know for sure what they were eating, but we do know that the soldiers in Homer's poem would have encountered a vibrant civilization on Gortnya. They would have wandered bustling markets. They would have gathered in citadels and temples. In Gortyna, the Minoan culture was rich, beautiful, and thriving.

9. The ruins of Gortnya still stand today.

However, in the 16th century BCE, there was a terrible earthquake, remember? The civilization recovered, only to be decimated by a volcanic eruption! Pumice and ash shot into the air, and a tsunami smashed into the beaches, leaving death and destruction behind. The markets were demolished and the citadel pummeled. The Minoan culture, once thriving in Crete, was in ruins.

As archeologists dig through the layers of history, more and more questions arise. Was it the natural disasters that caused the downfall of the Minoan culture, or was it an invasion? Was it Zeus, or was it Athena?

No one really knows, but we can make educated guesses based on what we find. And, in the end, we know the result. With the Minoan fleets decimated, the Mycaneans took over Crete, and another story began.

The Mycenaean Civilization would soon be followed by another, and then another, from one culture to the next. My island is a series of stories — some told in words and some told in the pottery and pieces left behind.

The Palace at Knossos

One important place from my story still exists: The palace of Knossos. The palace was the home of King Minos, and the site of the labyrinth, which was my home and my prison.

They call Knossos Europe's oldest city. Archaeologists have found remains of civilizations there from before 7000 BCE. Can you imagine? There were palaces on the hill at Knossos long before the current one, which dates to around 2000 BCE (which is still super duper old).

10. The Palace at Knossos still stands, pillars stretching to the sky.

The Labyrinth

Fine, I know. You want to hear about the labyrinth. Who cares about some broken down palace? Just a bunch of old kings like Minos lived there. Total losers. The labyrinth is the real wonder of the Ancient World.

Even if you are standing on the hill at Knossos, you can no longer see the labyrinth. It has moved into memory and legend. Historians question if it ever really existed...if I was even real. If they were standing next to me right now, I'd bonk them on the head.

Just kidding. I learned long ago that violence is not the answer. You have to change people's hearts, not break their faces.

I would instead show them images of me in museums and libraries, winding my way through history.

11. Here I am, engraved in this 16th century golden pendant. You could really get lost in this maze.

I would tell them the story of the labyrinth, and how people have represented it throughout history. The labyrinth wound its way, endlessly confusing and confounding. Some people said it drove infinitely forward along one path, while others represented it as a maze, with many possible paths to confuse and baffle the wayward traveler.

I would tell them about the labyrinths stamped into the coins in 5th Century Crete. How the maze was such a central symbol to many ancient people. I'd explain how Pliny wrote about the Cretan Labyrinth in the first century, along with three other labyrinths that dotted the ancient landscape.

I would also tell them how the Palace itself was described as labyrinthine — how there were so many rooms and twists and turns that maybe the palace was a labyrinth itself.

But I would mostly tell those non-believers to stop thinking so much with their heads, and lead with their hearts. Imagine a world where the labyrinth existed, how it rose up in the desert sun to become a myth, a legend, a story that was told across time and space.

Don't worry about the truth, or what's real and what's not. Sometimes, the story itself is more important than the evidence left behind.

A few words about words

The Minoans did have their own form of writing. In fact, Archaeologists rejoiced when they found tablets overflowing with scrapes and scratches forming symbols: ancient words, carved by hands, long ago. Historians hoped they could learn more about the Minoan culture from the letters scratched into the stones. They got to work, decoding and deciphering the tablets. They labeled the Minoan alphabet **Linear A.**

However, after years of studying and investigating, historians still have no idea what the words mean. They can't decode the alphabet.

It could be an ancient recipe for ambrosia, the food of the gods. Or, it could be a fancy grocery list. On the next page, you will find an engraved tablet, discovered in the palace of Zakros, near Knossos. Examine the words carved into stone.

What do you think was on their shopping list? Try making you own list using the letters below. What would you buy from the market at Knossos? What might you pick up in Zakros?

12. Ancient sandstone tablet with words scratched into the stone. What does it say? What do you think?

The thing is, you could only have visited the Minoan markets until about 1200 BCE. Some people say the culture ended because of the eruption, some argue tsunamis, and other say it was the Mycenaeans, who eventually inspired the Greeks. We can't read the stories the Minoans left behind. The tablets are full of words we do not understand.

But that's okay because our journey does not end with those broken tablets. While my story began in Crete, it definitely doesn't end there. This is just the beginning.

3

THE CULTURE

I am a proud Minoan, an island Minotaur. I lived in Crete for the better part of my life, and the worse parts, too! But the Minoans didn't ever get to hear my story. They were not the audience for tales of Asterion, the mighty Minotaur.

The **audience**, the people who were listening to my story, was actually the Greeks.

Now, before we take a trip down the historical timeline, I want you to remember that story you told your grandma. Remember how you took out the blood and guts? Removed the boogers? Remember how you made your hero a smiling, ever-so-polite raven? And the villain was a fish named Alfred with very bad manners?

What? You don't remember that? Well, I do, and that raven was so very civil. Quite the bird, in fact! You are very good at telling stories, my friend. The thing I like about you is that you know how *the audience for a story always impacts the way you tell a story.*

The people who were telling stories about me were

the Greeks, not the Minoans. Let's talk about why that matters, starting with a little historical stroll down the timeline from the Minoan Civilization and over to the Greeks. Here's the weavy way we will follow:

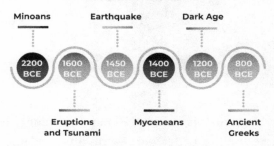

Crete Timeline

Minoans	Earthquake		Dark Age		
2200 BCE	1600 BCE	1450 BCE	1400 BCE	1200 BCE	800 BCE
	Eruptions and Tsunami		Myceneans		Ancient Greeks

13. So many things happened in the history of Crete, but here are some of the BCE highlights.

    The Minoan Civilization was thriving in Crete from 2200 BCE to 1400 BCE.

    Then came an eruption. BOOM! A tsunami. SPLASH! An earthquake. CRACK!

    What a string of bad luck. After years of natural disasters and destruction, the **Mycenaeans** (My-sa-nee-ens) arrived on Crete's shores.

    They were more warlike and a lot less peaceful than the Minoans. The Mycenaeans built palaces and bridges, dams and ships. They spread across the sea, bringing their culture across the Mediterranean islands.

    But the disasters were not quite over yet. The Mycenaean civilization collapsed too, leaving Crete in the Dark Ages for hundreds of years.

Hey! Who turned out the lights?

Honestly, we should have realized there was a big problem when the toilets stopped working.

It was all downhill from there. We call it the Dark Ages because society collapsed. Palaces were destroyed. The population decreased and trade ceased. The Mycenaeans became nothing more than a memory, etched in the sands and stones of time.

It's unbelievable, isn't it? Crete, which once had a string of thriving civilizations — with its own writing and coins and flushing toilets — was now a lifeless island littered with ruins of the past. First, the Minoans disappeared, and then the Myceneans. Whole cultures, gone.

14. Archaeologists pieced together amphoras and jars, revealing a very polite bird and perhaps even a fish named Alfred. The Mycenaean Culture on Crete was rich and vibrant, but disappeared. Archaelogists continue to sift through the relics, discovering more about this once flourishing culture.

Archaeologists uncovered pieces of the past: their bowls, their cups, their amphoras, and their palaces. They dug down deep to understand who they were and what they wanted. Most of all, they dusted off the relics to find out what stories lie beneath the rubble of history.

Questions still plague historians and archaeologists. Who were the Minoans? What did they want? What future did they imagine, and how did they disappear?

The Greeks

Here's what we do know. After years living in the Dark Ages, around 800 BCE, the Ancient Greek civilization sprang to life on Crete. They were like a light, blasting away the darkness, and they left a long trail behind them.

Archaeologists know a lot more about Ancient Greece than they do about the Minoans. Hop online, you can even read the writings of the Ancient Greeks (well, you would have to spend years studying their language first). They have their own alphabet, and we even know what it means! Instead of learning their ABC's, Greeks learned their Alpha, Beta, Gamma's.

15. Ancient Greeks, like the sculptor Phidias, carved words into stone.

The scholars of Ancient Greece scratched their letters on wood and papyrus, parchment and stone. They carved monuments and painted pottery, engraving words and wisdom into their everyday lives and down through history to present day. Today, Greece is a thriving nation.

The Greek people loved telling epic stories with heroes and battles and quests. After all these years, Greece is known as the cradle of civilization because it is where Western literature and philosophy were born, as well as the idea of democracy. By reading their words, we can find out more about who the Ancient Greeks were, and what their daily life was like.

Location

Mainland Greece is in Southeastern Europe. The Ancient Greeks traveled to islands, like Crete, eventually forming their own communities and bringing their culture to islands like mine.

16. *Part of Greece is connected to mainland Europe, but the ocean is also on its doorstep! Crete is the biggest island in the South. And the best.*

In your time, there are 227 islands with people living on them. Depending on how big you consider an island, Greece now includes up to 6,000 islands! The Greek people traveled from the mainland and settled on islands throughout the Mediterranean.

They also soaked in a bit of the island culture too, especially the food. Loo-koo-MA-daze!

Food

Yes, that's right. We are finally officially talking about food. My favorite topic (besides foot rubs). Once the Ancient Greeks arrived on Crete, they spent a lot of their time gathering food to eat and trading for other goods they needed to survive. While they brought some supplies with them on their ships, they had to find and forage for others. They were surrounded by the ocean, so what do you think was one of their main food sources?

If you said fish, squid, or shellfish, you are one hundred percent correct! Pat yourself on your muzzle.

If you said potato chips, tacos, or candy canes, you are one hundred percent wrong. Also, you're probably a little hungry. Head to the kitchen and get a sandwich before you read some more because I know this next bit will leave your stomach growling.

Ancient Greeks kept goats for milk and made cheese, too — delicious, bright, milky cheese that they scraped on breads and fruit. They were also good farmers. They tilled the soil, and grew olives, grapes, figs, and grains. If they couldn't grow or catch something, they traded for it. Their food came from the ocean and the soil.

Remember those rocky mountains and sandy desert-like landscapes in Crete? If you were lucky enough to own a little piece of my island, you focused on what might grow there. For example, olive trees grow well along the coast, but they hate freezing temperatures! So, if you were living halfway up the White Mountains, you would not be tending an olive grove.

What would you eat? Well, a farmer could raise goats

and sheep along the mountainside, and the animals could forage for food. If you had a goat, you could also drink goat milk (it's tangy, but delicious!).

Okay, are you ready for the most important question? DINNER! What would you put on your own dinner table in Ancient Greece? Would you fill your serving dishes with fruits and vegetables, or meats and cheese? Would you pour on oil or dip your bread in honey and salt?

In the space below, draw (or imagine!) your own dinner table. Write (or dream!) onto the placemats the foods you would eat. Here are some choices to get you started:

- Bread
- Beans
- Olive oil
- Fish
- Figs
- Cheese
- Apples
- Cabbage
- Grapes
- Honey
- Onions
- Loo-koo-MA-daze!

Work

The Ancient Greeks didn't just lay on the beach and eat grapes and write all day. They did more than draw tables: they had to make them if they wanted to eat at them! Life in Crete was hard work. For the most part, kids followed in the footsteps of their parents. If your dad was a fishermen, you'd get your own nets. If your grandparents forged axes, you would work right beside them by the fires. Take a moment and imagine living in Ancient Greece. What would your dream job be? How would you want to spend your days?

Would you be a farmer, planting crops in your field?
Would you be a weaver, creating fine cloth?
Would you be a blacksmith, forging sharp spears?
Would you be a poet, crafting epic adventures?

In smaller communities, you would have to learn many of these tasks to survive. You couldn't just head to the tailor to get your cloak fixed — you would have to mend it yourself. In larger communities, workers could focus on one or two tasks and trade or barter for the rest.

If you are a female, odds are that you would either be a homemaker or working in a temple. If you were a girl in Ancient Greece, you would have to run away to **Sparta** for more freedom. Women in Sparta could train like soldiers and do other tasks. Women in Greece, however, took care of the children and watched over their homes. Their lives were much more limited back then as opposed to today.

There are signs that Minoan Culture was different. In fact, there are images of women taking part in rituals and leading ceremonies. In other paintings, women can be seen participating in sports and just generally being in charge. Women had more power in Minoan culture than they did in Ancient Greece, which makes sense. My sister, Ariadne, would have made a great ruler! Plot spoiler: she becomes a goddess, so don't worry about her. She's totally in charge now.

War

In Greece, men had a lot more opportunities. Yes, they were fishermen, farmers, and blacksmiths, but they were also soldiers, trained to protect their cities. They were armed with spears and swords (though I personally prefer a nice club).

In the early years of the Greek civilization, wars were led by warrior leaders and part-time soldiers. Soldiers would bring their own equipment — meaning some had swords, some had spears, and you were lucky if you had a shield. You had to fight with what you had.

If you were suddenly called to war, how would you fight? Would you grab a pillow? Swing your video game controller? Ride into battle on your scooter?

When Ancient Greeks headed into battle, they fought with what they had. Later on, the wars were planned by cities and, eventually, states and nations. I know you've heard about the **Trojan Horse.** It was actually used by the Greeks during their war with the Trojans. Here's the deal. The Greeks had been in a ten-year long, unending war with the Trojans, when they suddenly got an idea: **Odysseus** (the famous Greek hero-king) and his men built a giant wooden horse, hopped in, and left it outside the Trojan gate. Then, the rest of the Greek army pretended to leave. The Trojans brought the horse into their city. What a cool present, right? In the middle of the night, Odysseus and his crew quietly opened up the horse, crawled out of its belly, and attacked the city. Hiyah! How do you like your present now?!

Sorry, I got a little sidetracked. What were we talking about? Oh, yes. Wars between cities. What? Like between Portland and Seattle? Or Los Angeles and San Francisco?

That's right!

The Ancient Greeks were less concerned with fighting for their country, and more concerned about protecting their city. Can you imagine fighting for your own hometown? Raising banners and marching to war?

What city are you from? Fill in the battle hymn below to create a song to accompany you on your way to battle.

Oh, _____
            City

Oh, _____
            City

Your banner we hold high!

We fight like _____
                    Local animal

Shout like _____
                  Local bird

And enjoy our _____
                      Local food

If you're from Portland, Oregon, you might have enjoyed some doughnuts. I personally just scarfed down some more Loo-koo-MA-daze while you were singing. My battle hymn from Crete also included partridges and bearded vultures. Birds soar through the skies in Crete and fill our treetops and our songs. I'd prefer to not go to war and just enjoy the ancient past-time of watching the migrating birds from the pink sand beaches of Elafonissi.

Government

While all Greek citizens shared the same language, religion, and culture, Greece wasn't as important to them as their city-state. A **city-state** is a city that had its own rules, laws, army, and coins. In short, each city-state had its own government that was in charge. That meant that a coin from Athens was worth nothing in Troy or Kydonia (a Greek city-state in Crete that was founded by the family of Minos. Uuuuuggghhhhh that guy again).

Moving on, your city-state was your home, and for the most part, you would live your life close to home, unless you were called away to war or trade.

Sorry, we're talking about war again! You see, sometimes these city-states even went to war with one another. In fact, the war between Athens and Sparta was a war between city-states. It was called the **Peloponnesian War.** Athens and Sparta were about 150 miles apart. Imagine if New York City attacked Boston.

Nowadays, the Yankees battle the Red Sox with a lot less bloodshed. The Greeks, however, spent a lot of their time at war, training for war, or thinking about war. It was a dangerous time to be alive, but a great time to be a hero.

Sing your battle hymn and grab your weapons! It's time to go to — wait, you need something to wear. I've got you covered (literally). Let's take a look in the war chest

for something to keep you warm during your trek over
the mountains on your journey to becoming a hero.

Clothes

The weather for training was always good in Ancient
Greece. In the summer, people wore lightweight clothing,
like a tunic, as the sun beat down. In the colder months,
they would pull on a cloak or wrap. Women's robes were
shorter, and men's robes were longer.

Their clothes were simple and homemade. Wealthier
citizens would dye their clothing and wear colorful robes,
but most citizens wore white or light tan. The Ancient
Greeks did not sew their clothes until far beyond my
time. Instead, they would take large pieces of cloth and
drape them over their bodies.

Sometimes, they would tie on a belt to hold it all in
place.

Can you imagine what their clothing felt like? Perfect
on a hot summer day.

But you know what...you don't have to imagine it! If
you are home right now, head over to your bed and pull
off the sheet. Wrap it around your body and tie it all
together with a jumprope.

You are now wearing a *chiton* - a sleeveless tunic.

Over time, the Greeks got really fancy about their
clothing, but I think you've got the right start.

Hey! I see one of you didn't even get up out of your
chair! How rude. There is a whole linen closet awaiting
you. Okay, fine, I'll make your life a little easier.

Let's do some drawing. First, look down at the shirt

you are wearing. How is it different than the clothing the Greeks wore? Are you wearing bright colors? Are the sleeves stitched on? Draw a picture of yourself below, or on a sheet of paper if this is a library book.

TAKE A LOOK AT YOUR DRAWING. IF YOU WERE AN ANCIENT
Greek hero, preparing to travel along the White Mountains to visit the temple of **Apollo** (god of the sun), what
would you wear? How might your drawing be different?

Draw yourself again below! This time, consider what
you would wear as an Ancient Greek on a long journey
over the mountains.

Wondering about footwear? You're thinking smart!
The Ancient Greeks wore sandals made of cow hide that
were fastened to their feet with lots of straps.

Concerned about carrying your food for the trip?
Well considered! The Ancient Greeks had small bags
they carried, too. Use your pen, pencil, or imagination to
give yourself better gear below!

Once you are ready, let's head off to the temple. The
journey is long, and the gods are waiting. Make haste!

4

THE RELIGION

When the Ancient Greeks arrived on Crete, they laid eyes on the remains of a great civilization: they found my people, the Minoans. The Greeks discovered the temples of the Minoan religion, and the palace at Knossos, and stacks of carved tablets. They found remains of statues and stairs carved into the mountainside. They walked through empty corridors of stone.

The Greeks must have been so confused! Who were these people? Where did they go? What did their carvings say? What did they do in those temples? How did they worship? And who were their gods?

Archaeologists and historians have continued to ask those same questions throughout history.

Minoan Religion

Scholars still don't know much about the Minoan Religion. Without history books (or *Mythwakers* books!) to help them sort through the fragments of time, much of what they know is based on pottery shards, broken stat-ues, and empty buildings. Minoan daily life is a mystery.

Can you imagine if all people knew about you was from your cereal bowl? Super terrible, huh?

Side Trip to Your Kitchen Cabinet

Take a second and open your kitchen cabinet (the one with all the dishes). What do you see inside? Bowls with cartoons on them? Big wide cereal bowls? Small, narrow bowls that are like cups? Do you have those cool bowls with the straw on the bottom to suck up your milk? Those are awesome.

Draw your favorite bowl below or on a piece of paper.

ONCE YOU'VE DRAWN YOUR FAVORITE BOWL, IMAGINE YOU are an archaeologist, and you just discovered this bowl in 4025. There is no written record of the civilization that owned this bowl! They know nothing about who you are or what mattered to you.

Consider these questions, and answer them below or on your paper.

1. WHAT COLOR IS THE BOWL?

2. IS THE BOWL PLASTIC? CERAMIC? GLASS?

3. DID THEY MAKE THIS BOWL THEMSELVES?

4. ARE THERE WORDS ON THE BOWL? WHAT DO THEY MEAN?

5. WHAT MATTERS TO THIS PERSON?

QUESTION NUMBER FIVE IS THE BIGGEST QUESTION OF ALL. You gather the **evidence** in the other questions and have to put it all together in that final question. Just like a real archaeologist, you would collect your evidence, and start the **scientific method** (a process for research).

Luckily, we can figure out a lot from a piece of pottery.

You see, history and archeology are actually like science and storytelling combined. You find the evidence and the pieces left behind, and you try to uncover what they mean — the story they tell.

Did the Minoans make their own bowls? One way you could figure that out is if the tools and materials that the bowl is made out of are available in the area. For example, as an archaeologist investigating a site in Crete, if you found a potters wheel with clay bricks next to it, and a bowl made of that same clay, you'd be *really lucky*. You could form a **hypothesis** (an educated guess) about that bowl. You would do some research, use your tools and scientific techniques to date and identify the bowl. After you had enough evidence to back that hypothesis up, you would check in with other archaeologists. What had they uncovered? Do their findings match yours? Why or why not? Archaeologists continually question and examine their research and findings.

Patterns

Archaeologists look for the pieces, but they also look for the *patterns*. What objects are we finding again and again? Where are we finding them? What do they reveal about the people who used them? Archaeologists sift through the evidence, looking for patterns that lead to the larger stories of the past.

For a long time, Minoan bowls featured a couple of particular themes. One theme was the ocean. Minoan pottery was filled with octopuses and squid and fish (maybe even a fish named Alfred).

17. Eight legs are wrapping around this pottery flask. I wonder if the archaeologists who discovered the pieces put it together one leg at a time?

When scholars pieced these vessels back together, they saw the flowing water and swirling octopuses, and they began ti understand that the ocean was a central part of the Minoan people's experience. The ocean mattered to them.

Minoan Goddesses

In the same way, as scholars walked the Palace at Knossos, they saw several other themes emerge. In particular, they found a statue of a woman holding a snake. That woman became know as the snake goddess.

The more they looked, the more they saw her! Historians have lots of ideas about her. Some think she stands for wisdom. Some think she represents life — growing and thriving, shedding scales like a snake. Still others think she represents mourning and death.

It's hard, isn't it? Looking at the past and finding out what it means?

The Bull

One thing scholars do agree on: the snake goddess was central to Minoan religion, as was the bull and its horns. The bull, in fact, was **sacred** — holy and connected to the gods. Minoans would use the bull in their **rituals**, which were ceremonies dedicated to the gods.

Friends, I was IMPORTANT in the Minoan religion. The people worshipped bulls, and even played the sport of bull-leaping. What? You've never played bull-leaping before? It's such a fun game! All you need is a bull and a powerful urge to jump. It's like leap-frog, but with a bull. Honestly, there's a lot more stabbing with horns and falling over involved. It's the best!

Just kidding. No humans were harmed in the leaping of the bulls. That would be cruel. In fact, bull-leaping continues to be celebrated in modern day France. It's called **Course landaise** (which is French and basically means bull-leaping). Crowds gather to watch the **toreros** (the bullfighters) dodge, leap, and dance around the bulls. They have a whole team supporting them, and the toreros are broken up into two groups: those who dodge and those who leap.

It's a dazzling sport, but seems a little unfair to me. Shouldn't the bull have its own team? A charging army of hooves and horns? I would jump right into those stands and cheer on the bulls.

Can you imagine yourself in Ancient Crete, filing into the bull ring, ready to watch your favorite torero?

18. The acrobatic bullfighter grabs the horns of the bull and leaps into the air! Huzzah!

Minoan bulls were part of the sporting culture of Crete, but they were also worshipped and celebrated. Artists painted bulls on palace walls, and archaeologists have uncovered more statues, paintings, amphoras, and even a gold signet ring featuring my fine horn-headed friends.

Women in Minoan Religion

Remember how we said that women held important roles in Minoan society? You can see that in bull-leaping paintings. Women stand (and jump) beside men as they entertain the crowd and challenge the bull. They must have been so courageous and brave! Standing before a bull and waiting for it to charge is a dangerous game. Add leaping and dodging into the mix, and, well, you would definitely need the gods on your side.

Or, I should say, goddesses.

The more scholars examine Minoan **artifacts** (old objects made by humans), the more they think that women played a significant role in Crete culture. Here's a (creepy) example: the Aghia Triadha Sarcophagus.

19. This sarcophagus had no lid, but the engravings are detailed and incredible. They remind me of the walls of my labyrinth.

A **sarcophagus** is a fancy coffin that you put in a tomb instead of in the ground. The Aghia Triadha sarcophagus is one of the fanciest you will find in Crete. Archaeologists discovered it in a tomb, and they think it's from about 1400BCE. Swirls of color splash down the sides, with circles and lines painted in reds and blues and browns. Why are we talking about it? The paintings cover all four sides of the sarcophagus, and many of them are of women. They are participating in religious rituals.

While the men are carrying animals, the women are clearly in charge. They are the priestesses. The leaders. They hold a place of honor and purpose.

I know. You just want to know if there was a mummy inside the fancy coffin. Well, get ready for the scariest possible answer I can offer you.

The sarcophagus was empty.

Some say it was grave robbers that looted the tomb. As for me...I believe them! Scary stories are not my thing! In fact, let's do one last review, and then move on to brighter subjects. No mummies. Ack!

To review: while scholars don't know everything about Minoan culture, they do know that the snake goddess was important, that women participated in rituals, and that bulls took pride of place. What's that? You see a bull getting ready to be SACRIFICED on that sarcophagus? You're wrong. Let's move on.

No more questions.

After all, when you look back that far, you can make a hypothesis, but sometimes the sands of time sweep the stories away or the mummies rise or the grave robbers come or...let's move on.

Is it Greek? Is it Minoan?

A lot of what we know about Crete comes from the Greeks in their stories and texts. But what matters to the Greeks isn't necessarily what mattered to the Minoans. For example, the Minoans focused on trade with other countries, while the Greeks developed trade along with war and conquest. In other words, if you met a random Minoan, she was more likely to trade you a fish for a taco. But if you met a random Greek, you might get that fish in your eye, or a wonderful taco dinner. Ancient Greeks and Minoans had very different approaches to life.

The same is very true about my story. In fact, a little bit of background about Greek religion will really help you understand the people who were telling and listening to stories about me. After all, the Greeks were the **audience** for my story — the people who were hearing, watching, and reading it.

So Many Gods

The big thing you need to know about the Greeks is that they had many, I repeat, MANY gods and goddesses. Their religion was all about the **deities** (dee-ih-tees), which is a fancy word for gods.

If I listed all of the deities in this section, you'd most likely fall asleep, or start crying, and we'd never get to the actual story. So, I'll trim things down to what you need to know: **DOTS**: Deities, Other worlds, Temples, and Stories.

Focusing on the DOTS is an easy way to look at religions from the outside, while trying to understand what the religion meant to the people on the inside.

Deities

Wait a second, just how many Greek deities are we talking about? Around 400 titans, gods and minor deities. The thing is, there were the big gods, and the little gods, but there were also nature gods that lived in particular places, and gods that protected individual city-states. Like I said, LOTS OF GODS.

That's the whole thing — when we talk about Greek myth, it's all gods and heroes (and heroes who had godly parents). This is NOT the case for other mythologies and religions. For example, Irish mythology has less to do with the gods, and a lot more to do with how the heroes were totally awesome (or totally not). Sure, there were gods around, but they were usually local gods. The stories were about the heroes: their homes, their people, and their epic battles to keep them safe.

The Greeks, on the other hand, tell sprawling tales of quests provided by gods and trickery dealt by gods. They tell of life granted by gods and death handled by gods. Their heroes travel to the ends of the earth and back again because a god told them to go on the journey...or tricked them into it.

Greek gods are distant, but ever-present. They live on Mount Olympus, and humans are like their toys. They play with them sometimes, and toss them away at other times. The gods are unpredictable, like a tornado or a summer storm. And honestly, sometimes the gods are not very nice!

You see, the mythology of a people is related to what is really important to them. For the Greeks, guess what? It was all about the gods. The gods helped them make sense of the world around them.

We call all the Greek gods combined the **pantheon**. We can break them down into 5 different groups:

1. Primordial Gods
2. Titans
3. Olympians
4. Nature Gods
5. Minor Gods (Don't call them that to their faces!)

Are you ready for Ancient Greek Pantheon 101 in less than two minutes? Let's do this! Grab your parchment paper and off we go!

Primordial gods were born out of Chaos. Chaos was there at the very beginning, then came Gaia, Tartarus, Eros, Erebus, and Nyx. These **Primordial Gods** literally formed the heavens and the earth.

Their sons and daughters, the **Titans**, eventually overthrew them. The titans, like the Titanic, were large, powerful, and, well, they eventually sank too.

The children of the titans were the **Olympians**. They represented different ideals and needs of the Greek people. For example, Aphrodite was the goddess of love and Poseidon ruled the sea. These Olympians created humans and both blessed and cursed them.

21. See? Even Zeus is missing his hands in this statue.

In Greek mythology, it is not always a good thing to catch the attention of the gods!

The **Nature Gods** include deities of growing things, along with gods of water, sky, countryside, and cities. Like I mentioned before, many places had their own gods they worshipped, so it was common to enter a forest and meet the god of those particular woods.

Not to mention all the nymphs! There were flower

nymphs and volcano nymphs and forest nymphs and ravine nymphs and...ZZZzzzzzz...

Sorry! I don't want to bore you to death! We haven't even talked about that yet and we're running out of time!

There were many gods associated with the world of the dead, the **Underworld**, like Charon the ferryman. He helped you cross into the Underworld with the help of nymphs. You see, nymphs didn't just play in nature, they also carried torches in the land of the dead.

Before you get too creeped out, I've got one more thing to say about the Pantheon: there were lots more gods. You knew that was coming, right? We can find ways to classify them, and if we can't, we throw them under the heading "**Minor Gods**," but shhhh! We never, ever, ever tell them that's where they ended up.

Gods are proud and selfish. They want our worship, they want our adoration, and they definitely don't want us to call them minor!

Phew! We made it! That wraps up Pantheon 101, and the D in our DOTS! Now, go get yourself a snack, and then let's head into the O: Other worlds.

Other Worlds

All of those gods had to live somewhere, and the Greeks imagined them living on **Mount Olympus** — the highest mountain in Greece, and the home of the Olympians.

Remember, mythology is the stories we tell about the past, and the stories of the gods helped people explain the world around them. They saw a giant mountain, and of course they told stories about the gods living there. It makes sense, right? The Ancient Greeks believed that their gods lived high above them, ruled over them, and threw thunderbolts down on them. Ouch! It wasn't the electricity in the air that formed lightning — it was Zeus. Zap! And he was angry. Look out! He lived on Mount Olympus, high in the clouds in halls of stone.

> *"...Olympus, where they say the gods have their everlasting home. No winds blow there, no rain wets it, no snow falls, but the wide air is clear and cloudless, and over it shines a radiant brightness: there the blessed gods are always happy."*
>
> *-Homer in the Odyssey*

If you wanted to talk to Zeus, you didn't yell up at the mountain. You went to a temple and the priests laid offerings on his altar, begging for his favor, near his giant marble statue. You could see his carved marble face, but he was far removed from you, living up on the tallest peak of the highest mountain.

The gods lived their best lives up there. Their food smelled perfect and tasted even better. They ate and drank nectar and ambrosia. You've never had it? Well, imagine the best thing you have ever eaten. Now multiply it by infinity and a billion and you'll get to the food of the gods. Pure perfection.

Some scholars think the ambrosia was like honey, sweet and syrupy. If you imagined tacos, though, I think you're fine. Gods have the power to turn honey into tacos anyway. Mmmm...honey tacos.

*22. Yes, Mount Olympus is a real place! Here is a
view of the home of the gods*

The gods lived high above the **mortals** (you humans). They reigned from far away in their palaces on Mount Olympus. The gods would not share their honey tacos with you, or their Loo-koo-ma-daze!

The Greeks saw their gods as distant and inaccessible. The gods would answer prayers when they felt like it, take what they wanted, and flee back into the sky. They were **elemental**, like the elements of the weather. They were wind and rain, thunder and lightning. They were immensely powerful and often very destructive.

Some cultures see their gods as personal and loving. For example, the modern Christian God is relatable and listening — he hears the prayers of his people and answers them. Zeus, on the other hand, answered when he felt like it, and often just got angry and threw down thunderbolts or sentenced humans to death. For Greeks, the titans, primordial gods and the Olympians were to be revered, respected, and feared. They created our world, but they definitely weren't part of it.

Into the Underworld

The gods lived on Mount Olympus, or far from it, in the depths of the earth: the Underworld and beyond.

Hades, the god of the dead, rules the Underworld. To get into the Underworld, you pay **Charon** — the ferryman — who takes you across the river and into the realm of the dead. When Greeks died, their friends and family would often place coins over their eyes to pay the ferryman for the crossing.

23. *Save up your coins to pay the ferryman. Recognize that cool bull on this coin? It's me!*

It wasn't easy to get into the Underworld, unless you were dead.

Otherwise, you had to get past the hellhound **Cerberus.** He guarded the gates of hell, keeping everyone out (or keeping them in, as the case may be!).

Once you made it past Cerberus, you had to swim through Acheron, the river of pain, or Styx, the river of hatred. You might even have to wade through Plegethon, the river of fire, or Cocytus, the river of wailing. If you were lucky, you swam through

24. *Every one of Cerberus' heads growl and bark!*

Lethe after all that. It was the river or forgetfulness.

It was also believed that the river Styx would give you invincibility. One famous hero — **Achilles** — was dipped in the river Styx. His mother held him by his heel, which meant his heel did not get dipped in! Oh no! His heel became his Achille's Heel — his vulnerability. He died in the Trojan War when Paris (the dude, not the city) shot him with an arrow in the heel.

Poor guy. That must have hurt!

The Better Part of the Underworld

The Underworld isn't all fire and wailing. It has two main parts — the Asphodel Meadows and the Elysium Fields. Most people, when they died, went to the **Asphodel Meadows**. It's the plain, old, boring afterlife for people who lived regular lives.

It's not heaven. It's not hell. It's just the Asphodel Meadows. If you did something truly heroic or great, you could make your way to the **Elysium**, which is also called the **Elysian Fields.**

In the Odyssey, Homer describes Elysium as the perfect place:

"No snow is there, nor heavy storm, nor ever rain..."

-Homer in The Odyssey

The only hard part is getting into Elysium. The judges of the dead choose where to send you. Are you made for Asphodel? Elysium? Or are you off to Hades?

The Greek judges of the dead are very...judicious. You can't get much by Rhadamanthus, Aeacus, and Minos (yes, Minos. UGH. You'll hear a lot about him. I can't seem to get away from him, Remember — I was even named after him! **Mino**-taur. UGH. So uncool).

The Much Worse Part of the Underworld

Far beneath the Underworld lies Tartarus.

Wait a minute. Isn't that also a dude?

Yes! Tartarus was one of the Primordial Gods. Weirdly, Tartarus is also a dark and gloomy abyss where the Olympians sent their parents, the Titans.

Remember Pantheon 101? Their parents super deserved it. Chronos kept swallowing all of us his kids, and tried to kill Zeus too. Super inappropriate. Zeus trapped him in Tartarus and scooted off to the majestic Mt. Olympus, to relax in style.

And that's the end of the O — Other worlds — for now. We have some Temples to visit (with a capital T).

25. *The majestic temples of Ancient Greece still rise up toward Mount Olympus. Their pillars are strong.*

Temples

While they were hanging around on Mt. Olympus, the gods would listen in to the prayers of their people.

Greek temples weren't like church — people didn't gather in the temples to worship their gods. Rather, the temples were usually devoted to one god, and they held statues or emblems of that god.

One example that you can still see is the **Parthenon** in Greece. It sits at the top of the **Acropolis**, an ancient **citadel** (that's a fancy word for fortress). The Parthenon, with all its marble columns, was built to house the **Athena Parthenos** — a giant statue of Athena. People would bring gifts to the goddess at the temple (like wool from their sheep). Priests and servants of the temple would make sacrifices to the gods, and all would hope that the gods heard their prayers.

26. *The Parthenon still stands in Greece, reminding us of the Ancient gods and goddesses, like Athena.*

The temples would often be decorated with images and stories about the gods.

Carved marble engravings at the Parthenon show the story of how Athena defeated Poseidon, and became the patron goddess of Athens. You see, the first king of Athens, **Cecrops**, created a contest to choose their city's patron. **Poseidon** (god of the sea) struck the Acropolis with his trident, and made a sea-water well, bringing the sound of the waves and the water to the temple. Athena thrust her spear into the ground and brought the people an olive tree. She was chosen as the winner. Apparently the king really liked olives.

Do you like olives? Do you pick them off your pizza or gobble them down?

If you're an olive-lover, you are probably excited about the olive-making. But just so you know: if you thrust a spear into the ground next time you are out of cooking oil, you won't get an olive tree or a well. You have to be a god to get those goodies.

That wraps up the T in DOTS! We've gone through Deities, Other worlds, Temples, and now it's time. Let's make our way to the final letter, my favorite part, the S which stands for Stories.

Stories

As you know, gods and heroes form the backbone of greek religion. For almost every big idea or theme in Greek mythology, there is a story to go along with it.

For example, wondering about fire? The titan Prometheus brought it to the people.

Thinking about apples? Hercules (also known as Heracles) has a thing or two to tell you about those.

What about bread? There are a whole bunch of gods that have to do with baking bread. They will tell you a story or three.

Hunger? Talk to Limos.

The seasons? Consider Persephone.

What's that? You want to actually hear a story? Well, let's get to it, then!

A little story

Persephone was the daughter of **Demeter**, the goddess of the harvest, and **Zeus**, the ruler of the gods. She was young and lovely, enjoying a summer day, out gathering flowers in the Vale of Nysa. **Hades** (Lord of the Dead) saw her and super fell in love. He kidnapped her and brought her to the Underworld. Um, uncool, right? If you love someone, big advice here: don't kidnap them. Not cool.

Anyways, her mother was devastated. She told Zeus that as long as her daughter was gone, the earth would not bloom, and everything would wilt and die.

Flowers fell to the ground. Trees shed their leaves. The earth died as Demeter mourned the loss of her daughter.

Zeus got super angry. If you've heard any stories about Zeus, you know that's not a good thing. He raised his thunderbolts and marched down to Hades. He demanded that Persephone be returned. Hades was all like, sweet. Yeah. Sorry. That was totally uncool of me kidnapping her and everything. Zeus gripped his thunderbolt and rolled his eyes. He knew Hades wasn't actually sorry.

Everything seemed okay though. Hades released Persephone, sending her back to the land of the living. But before she left, he gave her six pomegranate seeds. He knew that if she ate the food of the dead, she could not return to the land of the living.

27. *Persephone, seated on her throne, without any hands, either!*

She was starving, and popped them in her mouth, crunching on their sweet seeds. When she tried to cross over, her body froze. Her hands shook. She was stuck in the Underworld.

When Demeter discovered what Hades had done, she was beyond mad. The rest of the flowers died. The crops were covered in snow. The people froze as Demeter wept.

Zeus gritted his teeth. He couldn't change the rule of the land of the dead, but he could propose a compromise.

Persephone would stay in the Underworld one month for each seed she had eaten. That means that half the year, the flowers would bloom and life would thrive on earth, but when Persephone heads into the Underworld, Demeter is again filled with despair, and the world wilts and dies.

Great story, right? What did you learn?

I learned to not take any food for the lord of the

Underworld. He's totally a jerk. I also learned that Zeus makes super unfair compromises.

But, beyond all that, we can see that the Greeks told these stories to explain the world around them. They knew that there were seasons, and the world changed around them in cycles, but they didn't know why. Their gods, their heroes, and all their stories, were a way of *explaining the unknown* and beginning to understand it.

The story also reveals what the Greeks saw as important — compromise — coming to an agreement.

But more than that, the story reveals that the Greek gods kind of did whatever they wanted. They kidnapped, stole, tricked, and wielded their power to achieve their own ends.

Humans suffered the consequences.

The stories of the Greek gods revealed that the world was harsh and unpredictable, just like life for the Greeks. Only the strongest survived, and that's why stories of heroes thrived in Ancient Greece. They were powerful symbols for the Greek people to follow and admire.

DOTS

We have now connected all the DOTS! You have a much better understanding of Greek religion and the world of the gods, and I bet you have some opinions on Zeus and that loser Hades. Keep thinking about the stories you have heard as we explore a few of the characters that made their way into my own story.

5

THE CHARACTERS

Finally! We get to talk about me. You know how long I've been waiting for this? Just a few thousand years. It's about time!

You already know what I look like (I have hands!), but let me tell you a little bit more about my history and my family. Let's take a quick climb up my family tree.

28. Here is an early painting of my mom and me! Pasiphae was warm-hearted and wonderful.

You see, my mom is **Pasiphae** (puh-si-fay-ee). She was married to King Minos (ugh, that guy again). Minos was my stepdad, and he was totally a comic book villain, but not the cool kind. He had absolutely no class. He wanted the gods to send him a sign that he was the rightful ruler of Crete. He wanted everyone to know that he was the king. He prayed to Poseidon, the god of the sea.

Well, he sent offerings to the temple and the priests did the actual praying. But the offerings worked!

Poseidon sent him a majestic snow-white bull to sacrifice in his name — the **Cretan Bull.** The bull gleamed in the Mediterranean sun. Luckily, Minos didn't sacrifice it. That's the only good thing he's ever done. Trust me.

But...it was also a super bad thing. Minos bragged about how he had this epic bull and showed it off to everybody, which made Poseidon god-level angry. Minos was supposed to sacrifice the bull, not parade it down the street, showing off its horns.

Remember what we said about the Greek gods? You definitely don't want to make them angry.

Poseidon was like the waves crashing against the rocks — his anger and justice was swift. He punished Minos by making Pasiphae fall in love with the bull.

To repeat, he made my mom fall in love with the Cretan Bull. Weird, right? Gods are annoying. Always meddling in the lives of humans. The punishment was totally unfair, by the way. Poseidon punished Minos' wife because Minos was being pig-headed. Why not just punish Minos, the dude who was being uncool?

Anyways, Mom was totally head over hooves for that bull. Her love was like the waves crashing against...the Cretan Bull. To repeat: super weird. I wonder if Poseidon had some help from Aphrodite and Cupid? Only the Ancient Greek Love Team could create desire like that. Mom was all gooey-eyed.

With Cupid's arrows firmly lodged in her heart, Pasiphae gave birth to me. With the Cretan Bull as my dad, and Pasisphae as my mom, I was born half-monster and half-man, but still one hundred percent awesome. High hoof! Yeah! That's me! The Minotaur.

And King Minos, by the way, was still a total jerk. He trapped me in the labyrinth for thousands of years. Me! An immortal!

Don't worry — we'll get to that later. But it's still a good time to say: Uncool, dude. Uncool.

Minos

Fine. We'll talk about my stepdad. Ugh. Here we go.

Minos was the tyrant king of Crete. He was the son of Zeus and Europa, which should have made him wicked awesome, right? But it totally did not. It just made him actually wicked. He was the WORST. Every nine years, he forced the Athenian ruler, King Aegeus, to send seven boys and seven girls into the labyrinth to die. He forced them to sacrifice their kids.

29. *After his death, Minos traveled to the Underworld, where he lounged around with snakes. Seems about right.*

How did they die? I don't know. Hurricane? Tornado? Maybe they slipped in tacos and bonked their heads?

Fine, fine. I will tell you the truth. I wasn't always such a great guy. I mean, I was really mad for a long time. My stepdad had trapped me in a labyrinth for all eternity!

And then all those little squirts would come barging in, swinging swords and singing their own battle hymns, and sometimes, maybe, well, I got so annoyed about how they were singing about peacocks that I would eat them.

I'm not proud of that, but I mean, come on: one of them was singing a battle hymn about fighting like a flamingo and how he was going to rip me apart like a hedgehog. There's only so much a guy can take.

ANYWAYS, Minos forced Daedulus to make the labyrinth and trap me inside. So, Minos is a jerk. He's always forcing people to do things. Daedulus is pretty okay, though.

Daedulus & Icarus

Daedulus (Day-duh-lus) was a skilled craftsmen and architect. He created many beautiful and wonderful things — he was always using his imagination to think outside of the box, even when he got trapped in a maze of his own making.

Minos forced Daedulus to build the labyrinth, but once he was finished, Minos tricked him! He trapped him inside with his son, **Icarus**, and a very angry monster: me. Like I said, I wasn't the best guy at that time, but clearly Minos is worse, even though he wasn't eating people.

Eh-hem.

Daedulus wanted to free his son from the (not so a-maze-ing to him) labyrinth.

So he built Icarus beautiful wings of wax and feathers. Daedulus figured that even though he couldn't escape, he could still save his son. But then the saddest thing ever happened. Icarus flew too close to the sun, and the wax melted. Icarus fell into the ocean and died.

They renamed that part of the ocean after him — the Icarian Sea. You can still find it on maps and globes to

30. *In this illustration, you can see Daedulus flying away from the labyrinth, while Icarus reaches for the sun. The wax melts and his feathers fall.*

this day. The Icarian Sea splashes against the Cretan sands, full of memories and loss.

Daedulus was devastated. He went on to build other things, but he never got over the loss of his son — the boy who flew.

Side note

What did you learn about the story of Icarus? Take a second and think about it. Your grandpa might tell you that the story is about listening to your parents. Your dad might tell you it's about how the things you create can also destroy you (which is a little dark, Dad).

I think it's about Daedalus' love for his son. He adored Icarus. I think the story also explores what it means to be a parent. You see, even when you do everything you possibly can do to help your kids, sometimes, they do not listen to their parents (Except you, right? You always listen to grown-ups. Hey. Stop laughing. Go to your room. Fine. Keep reading).

For the Greeks, the story of Daedulus and Icarus was about all the themes above.

But the story was also about how the gods were always meddling in the lives of humans, and humans are sometimes trapped in situations they cannot control. Sometimes, those situations were created by men like

Minos. Other times, they were created by the gods, who were TERRIBLE, HORRIBLE, AND NOT VERY NICE.

Theseus

Speaking of terrible, I know everybody wants to hear about this next guy. **Theseus** (Thee-see-us). The hero. The dude who slayed the Minotaur. Blah, blah, blah.

That moron Theseus has been telling my story wrong for centuries. But I can't tell you the story you've been missing without talking about the golden boy from Athens, so let's get to it.

Theseus had a big ego because his dad was the King of Athens, **Aegeus**, and his mother was **Aethra**. Theseus wanted everybody to call him PRINCE Theseus. I think we should all call him LOSER Theseus.

I'm sure your parents would say that's super not nice, though. So, let's just call him Theseus. Ugh.

Just like Hercules, Theseus did a lot of heroic stuff. Unlike Hercules, Theseus was a total jerk.

Sorry, I'm letting my emotions tell the story. Let me take a deep breath, and remember that all this happened hundreds of years ago and I am a better bull now and I don't need to be mad at him anymore.

Okay, I'm good. Here we go.

What I meant to say is that Hercules had twelve labors and Theseus had six because he's not as cool.

What? I'm not mad! I'm just being honest.

You see, **labors** are important tasks that heroes have to do: usually defeating monsters or outsmarting bad guys. In Greek mythology, heroes were sent on these epic quests, called labors, to win the favor of gods and save their cities. For Theseus and Hercules, they weren't just fighting one bad guy. They were fighting several wicked monsters and villains, one after the other, on the way to complete their quests.

Greeks loved listening to stories about heroes, so Theseus was their man. And he did do some epic stuff, like defeat a wild pig. OINK!

To be fair, that sounds way easier than it actually was. Some people say that the **Crommyonian Sow** (that's the pig's fancy name) was the child of the monster Echidna and the giant Typhon. Theseus really b-oinked him on the head.

31. I do look pretty fierce, emerging from the darkness to...skip stones with Theseus.

The Crommyonian Sow was just one monster that Theseus defeated on his way to meet me. He also beat a guy that was conking people with a club and tricked a dude that was tearing people apart with pine trees.

Okay, seriously, his tasks were a little weird. Not as cool as Hercules at all.

Focus, Asterion. Focus.

The Athenians didn't notice how weird his labors were. When they told stories about Theseus, they focused on how he was smart and brave. He was from Athens, and he was their hero, their champion.

But, just so you know, the Greeks didn't always love Theseus. Later on, far after my story ends, the Greeks started telling stories about Theseus where he did some very unheroic stuff. He kidnapped Helen of Troy, and helped his best friend Pirithous in a plot to steal Persephone from the Underworld (why is everyone always trying to kidnap Persephone?). Plot spoiler: it didn't work out, and Hades got super mad at him. That's right: he angered another god! Not a good idea, but it was definitely a theme for Theseus. Ultimately, Theseus was rescued from the Underworld by Hercules, when he was finishing one of his tasks! See? Hercules *is* cooler. I can't help it — it's the truth.

Ariadne

There is one last person you need to know before the story starts, and that is **Ariadne**. She is my half-sister. While the ending of her story is quite distressing in this version, don't worry! Stories about Theseus get dumber, but tales of Ariadne get much better.

32. *Ariadne is on the right in this image (and she's not with Theseus!).*

After my tale is over, Ariadne eventually marries **Dionysus**, the god of wine. She has many children, and she becomes a goddess herself.

Things work out for her in the end, so don't let her part in this story make you sad. She gets what she deserves, and ultimately, so does Theseus (while she deserves the world, Theseus deserves a bonk on the head).

Speaking of stories, I think it's about time. You know everything you need to know. Let's get on with the story!

6

THE STORY

Finally, what we've all been waiting for — the story of me. I hope you brought your popcorn because this one is a hoof-biter (or nail-biter, if you weren't blessed with hooves like me).

Sit down, relax, and listen in as I tell you the story of Asterion the Minotaur.

As I was saying, you've heard my story before, "Theseus and the Minotaur." I hate it. I always get second billing to that jerk, and no one ever uses my real name. Well, not this time. Not anymore! This story is about the awe-inspiring, incredible, a-maze-ing Asterion, the hyacinth of the labyrinth! It is not about our gracious, glorious, golden hero Theseus—

"Did somebody say my name?"

"Theseus! What? Come on. When did you get here?"

"Minotaur! You hairy ox. I thought you were long dead! It's good to see you my old friend—"

"Friend? You literally tried to slay me with your spear last time you—"

"And I did. Slay you, I mean. I slayed you gloriously! Epicly! Your end has been told in songs and in stories throughout history."

"You did not slay me—"

"Yes! I did! Do you not remember? The beautiful Ariadne, and her winding string, and all the slaying? You were slayed over and over and over again—"

"Theseus! Just because you say something doesn't mean it's true! You have the story all wrong."

"Do I?"

"You do!"

"Well, then, you old bull, it looks like you have gathered an audience to witness, once again, your glorious defeat!"

"My defeat?"

"Yes! I, Theseus, the legendary king of Athens and its most revered hero, will once again slay you—"

"You did NOT slay me—"

"But this time, you will meet your end on the field of stories! Sally forth! Prepare your words. Sharpen your letters! Straighten your parchment. Your time has come. Again!"

"Fine. Fine. I was going to tell my story anyway. Now, I will just tell it better than you."

"Your words are dust. Your paragraphs are ash. You story will be slayed."

"Can we just get started?"

"We can. We shall! To the death! To the glory! To the—"

"End?"

"Yes, and to the end."

DEAR READER,

Yes, I'm talking to you! In this next section, you will read the stories of Theseus and Asterion.

On the left pages are Theseus' story.

On the right pages are Asterion's.

You can read all the left pages first and follow Theseus, or read all the right pages first (which Asterion will love).

It will be confusing to read them in the regular order, but either way, you will see that the stories have more than a few things in common.

Prepare yourself!

Read carefully, and discover more about Asterion and Theseus.

Your friend,
Kate

P.S. Thanks for reading this book.
P.P.S. I hope you're loving it!
P.P.P.S. This next part is the best.
P.P.P.P.S. Enjoy!

Theseus

I was born to be a king, and I died a king. My story is the hero's journey.

It all began the day I was born. I was destined to be a great hero from the very start.

King Aegeus of Athens, my father, was a just and righteous king. He had no sons, so he went to an oracle, who said I would ascend to the heights of Athens.

At the same time, the oracle said it in a super vague way, like oracles do. The King went to his friend in Trozinia for help figuring it out. His friend was like, hey! You should totally marry my daughter, Aethra. King Aegeus said yes, and nine months later, I was born.

Poseidon might argue with you about who my dad really is, though. Turns out Poseidon took a little walk with my mom on her wedding night. I'm kind of a god.

"Seriously, Theseus? You're calling yourself a god?
"Of course! I'm smart, fast, strong, and I slay things all the time. Who wouldn't worship me?"
"Wait until they hear about Persephone."
"Shh. I'm trying to tell a story here."

So, it's super clear I was totally always this awesome. Before Aegeus returned to Athens, he hid his sword and sandals underneath a giant rock. He told my mother not to tell me who I really was until I was strong enough to move that boulder.

And that is where my story really begins: the day I picked up that rock.

Asterion

I was born half-monster and half-man. My story is full of endless twists and turns.

It all began when the Cretan King Minos lost his son, Androgeus. He was killed in Athens.

King Minos was a horrible tyrant, incredibly cruel. He begged the gods to send a plague down on Athens. Thousands of men, women, and children suffered and died.

At the same time, his people were starting to question his right to be the king of Crete. I mean, who would want that guy in charge? So Minos prayed to Poseidon, asking him to send down a snow-white bull. Minos would sacrifice the bull and show that he was favored by the gods.

Poseidon sent the bull. It was gorgeous – strong and muscular, with long white flanks and elegant horns. It was clearly sent from up above.

> "Isn't that bull your dad?"
> "I'm getting there."
> "That's weird."
> "So is your face."

Minos' prayers were granted, but he didn't sacrifice the bull. He kept it for himself! Can you imagine? What a mistake. Seriously, never mess with the gods. Poseidon was so mad, he made King Mino's wife, Pasiphae, fall in love with the bull. Cupid shot an arrow straight into my mother's heart, beginning a song of endless love.

And that is where my story truly begins: my mother's songs.

Theseus

I put on the sandals and grabbed the sword. I was a prince and destined to be a great king.

I took the long route to Athens – monsters and madness. What other route could a hero take? Labors awaited! I would prove my worth on the field of battle.

> **"You were never in a battle."**
> **"Quiet, bull! They will hear of my glories."**

I was hungry – like the sun burning bright in the sky.

One day, Periphetes (Per-if-it-tees) attacked me with his club. I pounded him into the ground.

One of my proudest moments.

The robber Sinis met a similar fate. I slayed him too.

"I've got you now!" Sinis yelled.

"Give up!" I yelled back. "Stop trying to rob me. I will slay you four times over! I am a prince of Athens. One day, I will be king! You are my loyal subject."

Sinis shook his head. "I am no one's subject! I will pull down these pine trees, tie you to them, then let them go and launch you straight to Hades."

"Your strategy is to kill me me with some pine trees?"

"You're Tree Toast, Theseus!"

> **"That is a terrible battle cry."**
> **"I know! He should have sang of peacocks."**

I didn't want to be Tree Toast, so I bonked him on his head and tied him up instead.

Asterion

My mother sang to me of the stars in the sky and the horns on my head. She chased after me as I tested out my hooves, and picked me up every time I fell. She didn't care that I wasn't all human. I was hers.

But even though I was part-man, I was still a ravenously hungry monster. If I ate the food of men, my stomach would growl, growl, roar! At the same time, I couldn't eat the grass or the hay they fed to the cows. Chew. Chew. Bleh! I couldn't handle the fields of cattle.

I was hungry — like stomach roaring hungry.

One day, a thief broke into our fortress. In a fit of rage, I...um...I ate him.

> **"You ate him?"**
> **"I'm trying to tell a story here."**

Not exactly my proudest moment.

My father walked in just as I was flossing my teeth after my snack.

"You can't just eat people!" he said.

"It's not my fault!" I yelled. "The guy was trying to rob us! He killed four of our soldiers!"

Dad shook his fist. "And you were not any better! Roaring. Gnashing your teeth. Throwing bones across the courtyard. This is madness. Let the soldiers handle it, Asterion."

"I did!" I snapped. "And the thief killed them!"

He threw up his hands and charged out of the throne room. "You're a monster!" he yelled.

Theseus

Turns out, nobody ever wants to be Tree Toast.

That was gross.

Quietly, I picked up my sword and left the forest. These labors weren't so bad after all. Four more to go.

The next task was a real stinker. Literally. I could smell that sow for miles.

The Crommyonian Sow charged down the path toward me. "Oink! Oink! Oink!" I pulled out my sword, but felt my coin purse drop to the ground. I spun my sword around to catch the sneaky thief, and there was Phaia – that atrocious female robber – with her hands on my cash!

I wish I had known her plans. No sooner had I grabbed my purse, then the sow plowed into me. It was a gigantic, stinky monster!

I nearly screamed, but I got control of myself. I relieved it of its head and threw Phaia all the way to Tartarus. Sigh. Why were there so many thieves on the road to Athens? Seriously, being a hero is a full-time job with terrible benefits. Yes, there are epic battles, but there are also smelly pigs and so many angry ladies.

It was dangerous! But I was slaying all my labors. Luckily, I am strong and incredibly fast.

Also, super smart. When Scyron asked to wash my feet, I knew something was up. I asked to wash his feet instead. I'm tricky. With great cunning, I threw him off the cliff. He landed with a splash. "You didn't have to do that!" he yelled, paddling his arms like a giant puppy.

"Go away!" I yelled.

Asterion

Turns out, I wasn't the real monster.

That was Minos.

Quietly, he ordered Daedalus to build a gigantic labyrinth, with sandstone walls that spun for miles through the hot desert sun. Daedalus and his son, Icarus, worked furiously to complete the maze.

All the while, the people in Athens were suffering – they were dying. Remember that plague? Yeah, it was still going on, and King Minos wasn't letting up. Athens was dying.

Finally, King Minos relented, and ordered Athens to send him seven daughters and seven sons as a sacrifice. I wish I had known his plans. I wish I had known who those soldiers were. But all I knew was what Minos screamed at me – I was a monster.

I just couldn't get control of myself. What was wrong with me? I looked down at my hands. Yes – my hands. They were hairy and the size of dinner plates, but they were human, and they were mine. I washed my hairy face, scrubbed my snout, and ran my hand over one of my horns. They were razor sharp but couldn't cut me.

I was dangerous. Sure, I stopped the thief, but even when I did something right, I did it the wrong way. Maybe Minos was right – maybe I really was a monster.

I threw the wash basin off the table. It landed with a crash in the corner of the room. I stared at all the broken pieces. Mom was gonna be really mad.

I heard a soft knock on my door. I knew who it was. "Go away!" I roared.

Theseus

By the time I got to Eleusis, I was exhausted. I just wanted to take a nice long nap before the last day of walking, but an old man nudged me from my sleep.

"You're not safe here. He's a monster!"

"Who's a monster?" I asked, rubbing my eyes.

"Me!" he screamed. "I am Cercyon! Son of Agamedes! King of Eleusis! And your doom!"

I laughed. I couldn't help it. "Seems a little dramatic, don't you think?"

He reached out and slapped me in the face. "You smell like a pig. Wrestle me, hero. Or are you scared?" His lip curled into a smile. "I've never wrestled a pig before."

"I have!" I shouted, which was a weird thing to say, but I had just defeated the Crommyonian Sow and was still pretty stoked about it.

I defeated Cercyon with a single blow to his dramatic head, and then I took a long nap.

"Theseus. I don't think that's how it happened."

"Of course it is, you old cow! I absolutely slayed him."

"In a single blow?"

"Well, maybe two or three punches?"

"Cercyon wrestles. He doesn't punch."

"Here's a good strategy: try punching instead."

"I'll keep that in mind."

"Wait until you hear how I slayed Procrustes."

"What is crusty?"

"He was! After I slayed him."

"I walked right into that one."

Asterion

Ariadne opened the door anyway. She wasn't afraid of me. She looked down at the bowl, and then looked up at me. "What happened?" she asked.

"You're not safe here. I'm a monster."

She walked up to me anyway and put a hand on my shoulder. "You're Asterion. Your name means 'the starry one.' The heavens will bless you if you let them."

I laughed. I couldn't help it. "Bless me? How? With more horns?"

She reached out but pulled back her hand before she touched my horn. She knew how sharp they were. She smiled instead. "You'd look weird with three horns."

"I look weird now."

"Really, Minotaur, you could look worse. I once defeated the Colchis Bulls on my way to the Golden Fleece. They had horns and hooves made of bronze, but I slayed them. With my sword. Hi-yah!"
"Wait a moment. The Golden Fleece? "
"Yes! It was a gift fit for a king. Or a god!"
"Wasn't that Jason and the Argonauts?"
"No.
"I'm pretty sure—"
"Tell me more about Ariadne."

"We'll figure it out," Ariadne said, and sat down on the chair by my bed. She pulled out her weaving as I collapsed into bed.

"We always do," I mumbled.

Theseus

When I woke up, a tall, strange man was picking me up. "Put me down!" I yelled. "I'm trying to sleep here!" He laughed and dropped me into a tiny little bed.

"Do not be afraid," he said.

"I'm never afraid!" I shouted. I knew immediately who he was – Procrustes. I wasn't sleepy. Not in the slightest. Procrustes was a nasty dude.

"I have a surprise for you," he said. "But I need to make sure you fit. It's a nice warm feather bed to rest your weary bones. How about you relax, and I make you more comfortable?"

I knew he was tricking me. You see, Procrustes is notorious for plopping people in bed and if their legs are too short, he stretches them! If they're too long, he cuts them off!

Plot spoiler: we weren't going to take a nap.

I realized what was happening right before he raised his sword. I sprang from the bed, sword flying high.

I landed on Procrustes' head. Bonk!

I flipped him up and over me. Hiyah!

He flew through the air. Whoosh!

And crashed into the bed. Ploosh!

He was as big as a mountain, but the bed was full of feathers and so much softy stuff. He fell deep into the covers – it was an abyss of warmth and comfort. He struggled to get out. Ha! All those feathers were his downfall.

Get it? Down? Like feathers?

He was doomed. I had him right where I wanted him.

Asterion

When I woke up, there were men everywhere in dark clothes and cloaks. I reached out to push one away, but my hands were tied. I roared, and the man in front of me stumbled backward.

"Don't be afraid," a voice said.

"Dad?" I mumbled. I tried to rub my eyes, but my hands wouldn't move.

I wasn't sleepy. Not in the slightest. I was confused, and I was very, very mad.

"I have a surprise for you," he said. "But I need to make sure we make it out of the castle safely. I don't want anyone to get hurt. Do you think you can come with me?"

I should have known he was tricking me. He was usually angry, or yelling. And that night, he sounded totally reasonable, like we were going for tacos.

Plot spoiler: we weren't going for tacos.

I realized what was happening right before they threw me into a pit. I jumped high into the sky.

I squashed one soldier beneath my hoof. Eww.

I bonked another one in the eyeball. Yuck!

I hit another soldier's tongue. Gross!

And I tripped as I fell into the pit. Ouch!

I grabbed two of the soldiers and dragged them down with me. They screamed as they fell and we all landed in a pile of shields and armor in the dirt.

As they scrambled away, I looked up at dad. He was staring down at me; his face was like stone.

"Dad!" I yelled. He walked away.

Theseus

Then, I totally stretched him. Or whatever.

> "Wait a minute. You stretched Procrustes?"
> "Completely. Payback and all that. He was always stretching people and stuff."
> "How did you stretch him?"
> "With my mighty arms!"
> "You let him go, didn't you?"
> "No!"
> "Theseus, come on. Tell the truth."
> "He was tired! He needed a nice long nap."
> "So, you...?"
> "Pushed his bed on down the river."
> "And told everyone you stretched him?"
> "No, everyone just assumed—"
> "Because you told them?"
> "Yeah..."

"Take that!" I yelled.

Then I walked away. Straight to Athens and on to glory. Nothing could stop me. Nothing could thwart me. I was a hero for the ages. Who could defeat me?

Turns out, someone could.

After all this time, I still can't believe it. You see, I was incognito – in disguise. But my stepmother, Medea, she recognized me from the get-go. I played dumb and tried to be nice.

But she took the bad route, and so did I.

She sent all those soldiers, too.

Asterion

Now, I know I ate some soldiers. Like two. Or seventy-seven. But, we all make mistakes, you know? And after all this time, I really think my so-called dad should have just gotten me some help. Like, a monster mentor, or at least someone to talk to about not eating people.

> **"See! You were totally eating people. That's scary monster stuff. Dangerous. Murderous. Angry."**
> **"You are making me murderous right now. Come closer to my horns. I'll show you monster stuff."**
> **"Let's just tell our stories. Stop interrupting me."**
> **"You interrupted me!"**
> **"As you were saying?"**

Sometimes I think there are no real monsters. Sometimes I think we're all just trying to be understood.

The Greeks loved telling my story because they knew the world was unpredictable and terrible. They knew there were things beyond their control.

If their heroes could conquer the monsters, if they could slay the bad guys, they could be a little more in control of what was happening around them. They didn't have to be afraid anymore.

Anyways, Dad didn't get me a monster mentor or take me to Monster Academy. He threw me in a labyrinth and locked the door, with the soldiers screaming from down below. He could have made a different choice.

But he took the bad route, and so did I.

I ate those soldiers too.

Theseus

No one else knew who I was, but Medea did. She wanted her son to be the heir, not me. So, she sent a stream of soldiers to attack me. I was angry! But I was the strongest. I defeated every pig she sent my way. Then one day, she came to my chambers. She said she had an epic quest for me. She said I could save the world.

She was clearly speaking my language.

Okay, this is kind of turning into a whole big thing – me saving the world. But when you get really good at it, quests start to fall into your lap. She told me about the Cretan Bull—

> "My dad."
> "Yeah. Sorry about this part."
> "Really?"
> "Yeah. Sorry I was so awesome!"
> "Ugh."

Anyways, the Cretan Bull started it all. You see, the bull had trampled King Minos' son. Athens and Crete went to war, and Crete won. As punishment, the Athenians had to send a bunch of youth to the labyrinth every nine years as a sacrifice to the Minotaur.

They must have seemed like good snacks. He ate Athenian kids for lunch.

Medea sent me off to capture the Cretan Bull and stop his rampaging. Easy-peasy. I grabbed the bull by his horns, dragged him back to Athens, and sacrificed him to Apollo, which made Apollo super happy.

Asterion

I didn't even know who I was. I wondered endlessly through the labyrinth, scraping the walls, kicking down sandstone, searching for a way out. I was immortal — a monster created by the gods. My time in the labyrinth seemed beyond measure, like all the clocks were broken and I was infinitely traveling through the end of time.

Just like Charlie and the Clockbreakers!

I wanted to travel through time — go back to the moment I'd stood on the edge of the labyrinth. I wanted to destroy it all.

But I couldn't go back — couldn't change the future or undo the past. I raged against the walls of my prison. I crushed the sandstone beneath my feet.

One day, as the walls dissolved to sand beneath my fingertips, I drew the turn of Ariadne's face. It was an accident, but still, I could see it there, the way her chin tilted up toward the sun. I scratched another line, and then another, scraping into the soft stone. I laid down my memories of her and of my mother. I carved in the music that filled the palace halls — the notes that rose to the heavens like smoke and prayers.

I imagined a different future.

It was on those walls that I began to imagine a better world. I cut satyrs and fawns into the winding walls. With lighter lines, I formed water flowing through silken desert skies. In my images, it rained heavy drops of water from the sky. The rain gathered on laurel and cedar — a world beneath my fingertips.

The labyrinth gleamed with possibility.

Theseus

I've never met a stepmother who was so happy when I
returned home. She poured me a giant goblet of wine
and I raised it to my lips. In that moment, King Aegeus –
my father – finally recognized me. He saw the sandals on
my feet and the sword by my side and knocked the goblet
from my hands.

"You are a monster!" he yelled at Medea. He banished
her from Athens and pulled me into his arms. "My son!"

For years, we lived happily in the Mediterranean sun.
Well, except for my cousins, the Pallantides. They were
pretty mad I was back. They had wanted to take the
throne for themselves. You know, it's kind of a theme in
my life: People want to be me. But only I can be me, you
know? There's only *one* Theseus. Only *one* golden hero. I
captured my treacherous cousin just in time. "Stop trying
to murder me," I said. I raised my sword to run one of
them through, but my cousin waved his hands.

"Spare me," he yelled. "My brother made me do it!"

I turned toward his brother, who was shaking his
head. "Nuh-uh! I totally like you Theseus."

"You're awesome!" my other cousin said.

"We envy your awesomeness. Your bravery. You are
always going on epic quests. Being a hero. Totally cool." I
raised an eyebrow at them both. "We know you're going
to slay the Minotaur. Super slay. Totally slay. That's your
next big quest, right? You have really amazing...muscles."

I do have really amazing muscles. I wouldn't argue
with that. They were right.

Asterion

In those moments, I think I finally understood what it is to be human. I had spent so much time quietly raging or bonking and bashing.

I had never taken a moment for myself. To just be, you know? To breathe.

Maybe I wasn't just a monster. Maybe I was something more. Maybe I could be better.

For years, I had—

> "Eaten people?"
> "Yes. They know this. I told them."
> "Still, it's a pretty big thing."
> "You're not wrong...you want to say it one more time?"
> "Yes! You ate people!"
> "Are you done now?"
> "Probably not."

I made some very questionable decisions. Lived by my stomach. Followed my anger—

> "Ate people?"
> "Yes! I ate people. We went over this. Is time broken again? Why do things keep repeating?"

But I was starting to imagine a different future, one where I wasn't all monster. One where I didn't have to eat everyone who showed up.

Which is good because then I didn't eat Daedelus when he dropped onto my dining room table.

Theseus

I let my cousins go. Well, I punched them up a bit.

Because I'm a hero. That's what we do.

> "You punched them up a bit?"
> "I mean, I have a reputation to maintain."
> "...with punching?"
> "Didn't you eat a guy?"
> "Moving on..."

I knew what I had to do. The quest was clear – defeat the Minotaur. Save my people. Be awesome.

Sometimes, it's really easy being a hero.

I picked up my sword and headed to the throne room.

I didn't go in like, right away. I waited for a few more people to show up. What's the point of going on a quest if no one is there to see you leave?

Finally, when the bleary-eyed royal wannabes had all settled into their morning of annoying, I approached the throne. "Father," I said, "it is the Great Year."

"It is," he replied, filled with sorrow.

"Another year will pass with our sons and daughter murdered by the Minotaur on foreign shores. We cannot let this slaughter continue. We must end the Minotaur's reign of death. For Athens."

I practiced that. It sounded super good, right?

"For Athens!" my father shouted, and his attendants echoed his cries.

"For Athens!" they repeated.

Asterion

"Look out below!" he yelled. I roared in response.

Because I'm a monster. That's what we do. But the human in me watched the tiny bearded man drop onto my table with interest beyond rage.

"Who are you?" I roared. I meant to talk in a lower tone of voice, but I was in Monster-mode.

"Ah! Asterion! I hoped I would run into you. I'm Daedalus!"

I almost ate him right there.

He lucked out. Just at the right moment, I caught a glimpse of Ariadne gazing down at me from her carving.

Sometimes, it's really hard being a monster.

"Get off my table," I growled.

"Hear me out," Daedalus said. He was unclipping giant wings from his back. "Do you like them?" he asked. "They are my own design. I was trapped here once too. My son and I narrowly escaped your rage. The first designs...did not work as well. These are much stronger."

"What do you want?" He had built the labyrinth. I was seriously considering eating him.

"Seven years have passed. Once again, they send their sons and daughters into your cage. I beg you. Do not eat them. Set them free. They do not deserve your wrath."

I snorted. "I am done eating humans. But why should I let them live?"

"For Ariadne," Daedalus said. My breath caught at her name.

"How do you know her?"

Theseus

"We will send our sacrifice to the Cretan shores," I explained, "but I will hide in their midst. I will stop this madness. Our ship will leave with black sails. If I am victorious, I will change the sails to white and sail into our harbor with much rejoicing."

"Rejoicing!" the King said.

"Rejoicing!" his people repeated.

I set my sword at the foot of his throne. We could not bring weapons into the labyrinth. I would go unarmed. "For the glory of Athens!"

"For the glory," repeated in my ears.

When I arrived on Crete, all the ladies fell at my feet, including Ariadne. She was like, "Hey Theseus, you big, strong man. I'm going to love you forever because you're such a total beefcake."

And I was like, "Oh Ariande. You are super smart to love me. But I cannot return your love. Not right now. I've gotta go into that labyrinth. I can't stay with you."

And she was like, "Take this ball of string. It will lead you out of the labyrinth and back to me."

And I was like, "Awesome, lady. I'll totally come back and hang out with you. Because I love you. Just like you love me. I feel that way. With emotions."

"You're telling that wrong. My sister is smarter than that. She would never just throw herself at your feet."

"Love makes us do unexpected things. I can't help it that she super fell in love with how awesome I am."

"Ugh."

Asterion

Daedelus explained that they had sent Theseus to the Cretan shores. My sister, Ariadne, had fallen for him.

> "Told you. She thought I was awesome."
> "I still don't get it."
> "And I am. Awesome. Truly."

Ariadne had given Theseus a ball of string and a sword. Theseus would use the string to find his way through the labyrinth. The sword he would use to protect himself—

> "From you."
> "Or from your own idiocy."

What I tell you now is not in history books. It is myth and memory. It is mine — proof I am not a monster.

"Please, Asterion. Spare the soldiers. I will put on my wings and fly them out of the castle. I will save them, like I should have saved my own son."

"What happened to him?" I asked softly.

"I built him wings of wax and feathers. We had almost escaped. But he flew too close to the sun. He fell. And I lost everything. Don't make another family go through the same thing."

I paused, narrowing my eyes at this kind old man. "Help me escape," I said slowly. "I'm too heavy to fly, but help me find a way out of here, and I will help them find a way out too."

Theseus

Finally, I arrived.

Well, they kind of tossed me into the labyrinth through a hole in the sandstone.

But I was ready to finish my quest. The final labor. I unwound the yarn and followed a trail of carnage to the Minotaur's door. I grabbed a spear from the ground and pounded it against the rotting wood.

"Come out and fight!"

> "That's not how it went."
> "Is too."
> "You're telling it wrong."
> "So are you."
> "You had a sword."
> "I had no such thing."

The Minotaur opened the door, then shut it again. "No!" he yelled. "I will not come out. You are too strong!"

"You must fight, for it is I, Theseus! The great, powerful, loyal, regal, undefeated Prince of Athens! Prepare for your death, cow!"

That got his attention. He pulled open the door and roared at me. His breath was like a thousand dying snails. His feet reeked of stinky cheese. He was very hairy.

I stabbed him with my spear.

That made him really mad.

But I did not back down. I grabbed my spear and stabbed him again. My spear broke in his side, so I spinning kicked him right in his big cow head!

Asterion

History never tells you the truth. They say I ate the soldiers. Fought Theseus. Died on the end of his spear.

But I tell you true — I let Daedalus pick those soldiers up and carry them out of the labyrinth. I let him take them home to their families. To their friends. I let them live.

Even Theseus.

"Come out and fight!" he yelled.

I opened the door, then shut it again. "Go away!" I yelled.

"No!" Theseus yelled back.

"Please. I'm trying to carve a wall here. Go home. Tell them you won."

"I...can't. It's my last labor. I have to defeat you. Or I'll never become king. I am the golden son of Athens, your sworn enemy.

"I know. I'm the symbol of Minos. The Minotaur. By defeating me, you symbolically defeat your enemies. You need this as a culture. It part of your larger myth."

"Um...what? I just need your horn so I can take the throne. My dad said I should get it. To prove that I'm worthy. And I am. For Athens!"

"Why are you yelling?"

"Pomegranates!" he screamed. "Peacocks!"

I have no idea what that had to do with anything.

"If I give you a piece of my horn, will you go away?"

"Are you tricking me?"

"No."

"That's what a liar would say."

Theseus

He shook his horns, stunned, and turned to run. "You cannot run from me, you insolent bull," I yelled. "I am Theseus, the golden son of Athens. The light of the gods shines down on me. Turn around and face your doom!"

> "You were very insistent."
> "I had been running through that speech all day."
> "It was a long walk to my front door."
> "It felt like an eternity. I was lucky to have that yarn. The stories never explain how boring everything was."

The Minotaur spun toward me, a murderous look in his eyes. He was beyond reason. His great jaws chewed on bone that stuck out from his teeth like a toothpick.

"I curse you and all the gods!" he yelled. "I hate Apollo! And Athena! I am totally a bad monster. And I'm angry! I like to kill things!"

> "That doesn't really seem like me."
> "You never remember words spoken in the heat of battle. You were beyond your senses."

I knew what I had to do. I could not let this monster survive to murder more Athenian children. He cursed the gods. He smelled like old cheese. His time was done.

He had broken my spear, so I lunged for his club. I picked it up with my big, muscled arms and raised it high into the air. With a heroic twirl, I spun around faster than Hermes, and smashed the club into his meaty neck.

Asterion

I shook my horns, stunned. Honestly, it went on like that for a while. Him calling me a liar while I trimmed my horn. And don't worry. Horns are like toenails. It grew back in like a week. You humans get pedicures. Us Minotaurs get hornicures.

With one final cut, it fell into my hand. I threw open the door, just wanting to get him off my patio and back to Athens, when I accidentally knocked him over. He fell and bonked his head and was out like an eclipse — like someone had draped a blanket over the golden sun of Athens. I nudged him with my foot. He didn't move.

"That didn't happen! I fought bravely."
"Yes! You sang your songs of Athens, screamed about birds, and stabbed with your stabby spear. Heroically."
"For Athens!"

Just then, Daedalus arrived. Of course.
"Asterion! You promised!"
"He's not dead. I accidentally knocked him over."
"Thank the gods. He's very tiny."
"Yes, much smaller than I expected."

"No, I'm not!"

Daedalus picked up the end of the yarn. "This was really helpful. I followed it right back to the front door. It made for a much easier flight. Your sister is very smart."

Theseus

As the Minotaur toppled, his horn cracked against the sandstone and fell to the ground.

I raised it up in victory. For Athens.

"Good story. Are you going to finish it?"

"That seems like a decent ending."

"But we will miss the glory of your return home! How you took the throne of Athens. How you became king."

"It was a truly glorious moment. You are right, you old bull. I'll tell the story. For the glory of Athens."

I didn't need an army. I was a battalion! I slayed the Minotaur and followed the yarn back to the castle, where the soldiers pulled me up to glory.

Ariadne waited for me at the top of the pit.

"Oh, Theseus," she said. "You have muscles bigger than mountains and your brow is most magnificent."

She fell at my feet and started weeping. I pulled her up in my arms, and she begged to join me in Athens. We boarded the ship, her hand tucked under my arm. She cried as she waved goodbye to her homeland. She was really sad!

The Minotaur was nothing more than a memory.

Athens was victorious! The battles were over. Crete was ours. Everyone rejoiced at the death of the Minotaur. The beast no longer roamed the labyrinth, roaring to be fed and eating unexpecting children.

We began the long and treacherous journey home.

Asterion

"She is. I can't wait to see her again. When will you be back, my friend?"

Daedalus turned his head thoughtfully. "I've been trying to think of how to design wings that could lift you from the ground. But you are quite large and fearsome. I don't think my current design would work. I was thinking of getting a little help instead. I have an idea for an automated person. They could break down the walls and carry you to freedom. They would be like your own personal army."

"I don't need an army. I just need a way out." I followed the line of yarn disappearing into the distance. I knew where it led, but I couldn't get past the soldiers standing on the edge of the pit. They threw down rocks and I roared endlessly. That was not the way out for me yet. But it could be.

"I'll work on that." He had that gleam of creation in his mind. I could see the wheels turning. Daedalus was always an engineer, an inventor, and a good friend. "I'll bring you books in the meantime. Tomes to line your shelves and help the time pass. Myths and memories."

"But no stories of glory and battle, please. I want to know about the beginning of time. I want to read about Chaos, Nyx, and the Hundred Handed Ones. I want to learn about creation and new beginnings. I want to read about life, not death. I've had enough of war. I'm ready for peace."

"Me too, my friend. Me too."

Theseus

Our first stop was Naxos. While we loaded the ship, Ariadne went off with the women to look at flowers and be women together. When it was time to leave, they said she had fallen asleep. I was super sad, but I knew she needed to rest and I didn't want to wake up. I left her on the shores of Naxos and headed for home.

> "You left my sister sleeping on the beach."
> "I knew her destiny was to become a goddess. She is married to Dionysus now. They are really happy."
> "You are very heroic."
> "Thank you."

When we reached the Athenian shores, my men were overjoyed. We cheered and shouted, but oh, our joy quickly turned to sorrow.

I had told my father that I would raise a white sail if I was victorious, but my crew would heft up the black if I was defeated. I looked up at the sails and realized my error. We tried to change the sails, but we were too late. My father succumbed to grief. He hurtled himself off the cliffs into the ocean, and I became king.

We named the sea after him. Even now, you can sail across the Aegean Sea as you make your way to Athens.

When I opened the palace doors, the weight of the crown fell onto my head. It's hard being a king! But I think I did a good job. I united the city and built the first palace on the Acropolis. While some heroes remain myth, I became history - an early king of Athens. Huzzah!

Asterion

Theseus stirred on the ground, moaning about peacocks.

"You'd better get going," I said, handing him my horn. "The golden son will need this." He tucked the horn in his pocket and tied the yarn to Theseus' toe. His feet were covered in dirt and sand from the journey.

"This one will tell his own stories. There's no stopping him. Great labors. Defeating the Minotaur, following the yarn, saving the girl."

"He will. But we'll know the truth. And if it ends this war, I don't care if he screams about peacocks."

Daedalus lifted him up and shook out his wings. "Until next time."

I waved goodbye as the golden son rose into the sky.

I walked back into my house, shutting the door behind me. I looked at the walls inside, already covered in carvings of juniper and laurel. One space remained by the fire place. It had bothered me for longer than I could remember. Something big had to go there. Something important. I would see it every day as a I cooked my food or warmed my feet. I couldn't just carve anything there.

I stared down at my hands, then looked up with a smile. I went to grab my tools.

Theseus, the golden son of Athens was leaving. His memory would flood the scrolls of Athens. His stories would stretch forward in time, an unbroken line of faded truths and glorious deeds.

But I needed something more. Monster and man, it was time to sculpt my own story. It was time to carve the myth of me.

Asterion and Theseus

"Thanks for listening to my glorious story, you grizzled old bull."

"And thank you for listening to mine, you renowned and acclaimed, magnificent and swell, valiant and splendacious golden hero."

"Splendacious. I like that. I am splendacious. Listen, is your sister around?"

"No."

"That's unfortunate. I was going to show her my new crown. I got it from—"

"Get out of here."

"But you haven't even—"

"Nope."

"Can you give Ariadne my—"

"Roar!"

"Bye!"

7

THE MEANING

Okay. He's gone. Heroes are exhausting, aren't they? That's Greek Mythology, though. It's full of gods and monsters, and heroes on quests. They complete labors. They win fame and fortune and maybe even a crown. Everyone else is left sleeping on a beach or, you know, dead.

Why was this story so popular?

It's not surprising that Theseus' story was told over and over again. He became a hero for the Athenian people through the three O's:

1. Outwit
2. Overcome
3. Outlast

He outsmarted thieves that were targeting peasants and soldiers. He made travel safer between towns.

Theseus stood for our ability to OUTWIT enemies. Remember Procrustes? He was lying in wait on the road, ready to attack any poor traveler that came along. Theseus flipped his tricks right back on him. He made the people safer.

Theseus also represented our ability to OVERCOME obstacles and adversity. He went on a heroic journey, full of perils and labors. He defeated anything that got in his way, from beds to trees to giant pigs. I was the final labor he had to overcome before he became king. Just like Hercules, Theseus vanquished his enemies and completed his labors. He was a hero.

He also survived, and so did his story. Greek heroes OUTLAST their enemies. They overcome, outwit, and defeat dangerous monsters and scary things. People loved him because they didn't have to be afraid anymore. He outlasted his enemies, and his story lived on.

What did he outwit, overcome, and outlast?

- Monsters
- Thieves & Villains
- Labors
- The labyrinth
- The unknown
- Time

That last one really matters — he beat time through epic tales. You've read about Theseus and the labyrinth before, right? His story sticks in our heads because he represents what we want to be. They sang songs of his perils and recited poetry in his memory. He was their hero and their king.

The Journey

As you read more about Greek Mythology, you will hear all about the **Hero's Journey**. From cradle to grave, heroes follow the path of the righteous, defeating enemies and, you know, saving the world.

Over time, you'll be able to identify the different parts of the journey. You'll usually see:

1. The departure
2. The adventure
3. The return

Some scholars call number two the initiation.

You can see this structure in Theseus' story, right? He left Athens to go on his adventure. Remember how he wanted to finish his story before the return, when the adventure was done? I made him wrap up the story.

Scholars have also pointed out the **Heroine's Journey**, which has three stages:

1. The Descent
2. The Search
3. The Ascent

The story I was telling was very different than Theseus', right? Theseus was wrapped up in his journey — heading out into the world and defeating the enemy.

The heroine's journey is about community and connection. It is about becoming who you are — healing and hoping.

Make sure you head to Find Out More to read more about the Heroine and Hero's Journeys. They are a great way to understand stories and even write your own.

Why Theseus?

I've been thinking about this for a long time. Why did Theseus' story last? Beyond his hero status and ability to outwit, overcome, and outlast, why do we keep telling his specific story?

Athenians retold Theseus' story because he was their local hero. He saved Athens. He became the king. He moved from myth to history because they have him in their historical records as an early Athenian king. He wasn't just a memory, he was a recorded reality.

But, here's the thing: Hercules became a hero for the ages because his labors and trials were universal. Theseus' journey become more and more tied to Athens. He was a local hero, while Hercules came to represent all of Greece, and all of humanity (Shhh...don't tell Theseus).

Why the Minotaur?

I, on the other hand, came to represent monsters. Even when people forget Theseus' name, they still remember me. Why?

Because I'm a-maze-ing.

You walked right into that one.

But seriously, have you ever been lost, or faced a challenge that seemed insurmountable? Have you ever been overwhelmed by a project or homework or moving to a new town? The myth of the labyrinth is like that. The labyrinth was a place people did not understand, and it scared them. Add to that: there was a monster inside, lurking around every corner.

The unknown is frightening. Stories of danger and escape help us deal with those fears. They help us make sense of our world.

Labyrinths and mazes make their way through stories across cultures and time. The idea of being lost is something we all understand. The idea of being found, or finding our way out of the maze/jungle/cornfield/shopping mall, is also a feeling we relish.

We head into a corn maze for the challenge of finding our way out. When we can't find the exit, our hearts pound. Or when we can't find our friend, our palms begin to sweat. Finding our way out of a maze or escaping a monster is a situation we all connect with emotionally. We've felt the fears in smaller ways all of our lives. We want to find our way back home.

Another Story

For many of you, I represent the monster. I am your fears. I stand for everything you're scared of when you go somewhere you do not quite understand. I'm what you imagine in the darker places of your world.

But I don't have to be.

I hope, in this book, you were able to imagine a different story — that you were able to see things from my perspective. Not all monsters are, well, monsters, and not all heroes are heroes.

And honestly, one thing Theseus did not explain or dwell on is the fact that he had so much help along the way. He did not outwit them. Ariadne did. He also had a sword from the king to help him overcome, and sailors on his ship to help him outlast. They told his story and carried him home.

Theseus had the gifts he needed to succeed, and the allies he needed to win.

Heroes don't just emerge out of nothing and neither do monsters. We tell their stories. We create their futures.

As you leave the labyrinth and head back into your own world, I hope you carry Ariadne's yarn with you. I hope you weave a world of myth and magic. And whenever you need me, I'll be right here, ready to tell you a story again.

Until next time,

Asterion the Minotaur

P.S. You're a-maze-ing!
P.P.S. High hoof!
P.P.P.S. Don't forget to check out the cool stuff on the next few pages!

8

FIND OUT MORE

The best place to find out more about Greek Mythology is your local library! Ask your librarian to print out a book list for you, or bring them this one. This list is just the ones that Kate really enjoyed while researching this book. There is so much more to read and explore.

Books

Modern Introductory Books for tweens and teens (Go to your library)

- *Percy Jackson's Greek Heroes* by Rick Riordan
- *Gods & Heroes* by Matthew Reinhart and Robert Sabuda
- *The Olympians Series* by George O'Connor
- *Greek Myths* by Ann Turnbull
- *Treasury of Greek Mythology: Classic Stories of*

Gods, Goddesses, Heroes & Monsters by National Geographic

- *The Mythology Handbook: A Course in Ancient Greek Myths* by Lady Hestia Evans
- *Greek Myths: Meet the heroes, gods, and monsters of ancient Greece* by Jean Menzies

Modern Advanced Books Kate read years ago (Go to your library)

- *Mythology: Timeless Tales of Gods and Heroes* by Edith Hamilton
- *D'Aulaires' Book of Greek Myths* by Ingri d'Aulaire and Edgar Parin d'Aulaire
- *The Greek Myths* by Robert Graves
- *The Golden Age of Myth and Legend* by Thomas Bullfinch
- *The Complete World of Greek Mythology* by Richard Buxton

Modern Advanced Books Kate read recently (Go to your library)

- *24 Hours in Ancient Athens* by Philip Matyszak
- *Heroines of Olympus* by Ellie Mackin Roberts
- *Mythos* by Stephen Fry
- *Heroes* by Stephen Fry
- *Greek Mythology* by Liv Albert
- *A History of Crete* by Chris Moorey

Classic Books and Plays (Go to your library)

- *The Iliad* by Homer
- *The Odyssey* by Homer
- *Theogeny* by Hesiod
- *Medea* by Euripedes
- *Prometheus Bound* by Aeschylus
- *The Persians* by Aeschylus
- *Oedipus Rex* by Sophocles
- *Antigone* by Sophocles

On the Internet

Geography

- Basic Map: https://cdn.britannica.com/75/192875-050-86D61913.jpg
- Interactive Map: https://www.ancient-greece.org/map.html
- Sattelite Images: https://geology.com/world/greece-satellite-image.shtml
- Geography: https://www.ducksters.com/history/ancient_greece/geography.php

Crete

- Basics: https://kids.britannica.com/students/article/Crete/273850
- Advanced: https://www.worldhistory.org/crete/
- Timeline: https://www.worldhistory.org/timeline/crete/
- History: https://academickids.com/encyclopedia/index.php/History_of_Crete

Minoan Civilization

- Basics: https://kids.
  kiddle.co/Minoan_civilization
- Advanced: http://academickids.com/
  encyclopedia/index.php/Minoan_Civilization
- History: https://www.
  ancient.eu/Minoan_Civilization/
- Art: https://www.khanacademy.org/humanities/
  ancient-art-civilizations/aegean-art1#minoan
- Video: https://study.com/academy/lesson/
  minoan-civilization-facts-map-timeline.html
- Advanced Video: https://opb.
  pbslearningmedia.org/resource/
  thegreeks_ep1_clip02/thegreeks_ep1_clip02/

Mycenaean Civilization

- Basics: https://kids.kiddle.co/Mycenae
- Advanced: https://www.
  worldhistory.org/Mycenaean_Civilization/
- History: https://libraryforkids.com/
  mycenaean-greece-the-first-greeks/
- Art: https://www.khanacademy.org/
  humanities/ancient-art-civilizations/aegean-
  art1/mycenaean/a/mycenaean-art-introduction
- Video: https://www.youtube.com/watch?
  v=RZioHxDVCGE

Greek Civilization Introduction

- Background: https://www.bbc.co.uk/bitesize/topics/z87tn39/articles/zxytpv4 and https://kids.nationalgeographic.com/geography/countries/article/greece
- Clothing: https://www.historyforkids.net/greek-clothing.html
- Everyday life: https://www.bbc.co.uk/bitesize/topics/z87tn39/articles/zc8yb9q
- Food: https://historylink101.com/2/greece3/food.htm
- Art: https://www.ducksters.com/history/art/ancient_greek_art.php
- History: https://www.historyforkids.net/ancient-greece.html
- Religion: https://www.greekmythology.com/ and https://rickriordan.com/extra/meet-the-greek-gods/
- Music: https://www.youtube.com/watch?v=-1aAunaw1GA
- Video: https://www.youtube.com/watch?v=RchSJSJAbco

Greek Civilization Advanced

- Background: https://www.britannica.com/place/ancient-Greece
- Everyday life: https://libguides.spsd.org/greece/dailylife
- Food: https://www.saveur.com/article/Travels/Food-History-of-Greece/

- War: https://www.
  worldhistory.org/Greek_Warfare/
- Art: https://courses.lumenlearning.com/suny-
  fmcc-hum140/chapter/1-4-greek-architecture/
- Religion: https://www.theoi.com/
- History: https://www.ancient-greece.org/
  history/intro.html
- Video: https://education.nationalgeographic.
  org/resource/history-101-ancient-greece

Theseus and the Minotaur

- Basics: https://www.storynory.com/the-
  Minotaur/
- Advanced:
  https://pressbooks.pub/iagtm/chapter/story-
  theseus-and-the-Minotaur/
- Art: https://scalar.usc.edu/works/ancient-
  art/representations-of-the-Minotaur-and-his-
  story
- History: https://www.
  dailyhistory.org/What_was_the_legend_of_the
  _Minotaur
- Science: https://www.youtube.com/watch?v=
  2aoIs-5zqoI
- Video: https://youtu.be/gpVWMQ8g6K4
- Audio:
  https://www.stitcher.com/show/national-
  geographic-kids-greeking-out/episode/s2e1-
  theseus-and-the-Minotaur-69664391

- Texts: https://www.theoi.com/
  Ther/Minotauros.html

Over time, these links will become outdated. You will have to dig in and explore new research. Remember, librarians are your friends. They know where to find great resources — from books to videos to articles. If you get stuck, just ask for help! And even if you're not stuck, ask a librarian. You never know what wonderful worlds they will introduce to you. Read on!

9

SOURCES

Find out more about the photos in this book. No changes were made to any of these photos, and at the end of each of these descriptions, you will find a specific citation, which tells you more about where the photo comes from. It gives credit to the person who took the photo, which is really important for artists! It's also important for you — if you want to know more about an image, you'll find all the information you need to do further research. Read on to discover more about these photos of my world.

1. This image is called "The Minotaur, tondo of an Attic bilingual kylix." Say what? Well, a **tondo** is a round piece of art. The Minotaur is actually painted on a circular **kylix** - a drinking cup. You're going to see the word "**bilingual**" on a lot of the images of me. Bilingual means that you can speak two languages (cool!); it is also an art term. It's the fancy word for those Ancient Greek paintings that use both black and red/orange. When you're looking at old pottery, you'll also see the word

"**Attic**." That usually means from the Attica, which is a region in Greece. It has also come to mean this type of pottery-making. When you see "Attic," just remember, they're not talking about your house. You can find this photo from Marie-Lan Nguyen at Wikimedia Commons.

Source: Marie-Lan Nguyen, CC BY 2.5 via Wikimedia Commons

2. This illustration is called "The Minotaur." That's right — this one is named after me, too! William Blake (poet, artist, printmaker, creative guy) drew it in the 1820's to illustrate a scene from Dante's *Divine Comedy*. I thought it was a super cool drawing until I found out that it shows me as a bad guy in hell. Not nice, Dante (the drawing is still pretty sweet, Blake). You can find this drawing at the Fogg Art Museum at Harvard University, or online at Wikimedia Commons.

Source: William Blake, Public domain, via Wikimedia Commons

3. This engraving is called "Dante and Virgil meet the Minotaur." It's another illustration of me hanging out in hell (uncool, Dante). In fact, the lines beneath this engraving called me: "The infamy of Crete." Okay, that's a pretty cool nickname. The creator of this illustration, French artist Paul Gustave Louis Christophe Doré, is known for having a long name and for making wood engravings like this in classic books. You can find many more of his engravings at Wikimedia Commons.

Source: Scanned, post-processed, and uploaded by Karl Hahn, Public domain, via Wikimedia Commons

4. Time to put your thinking cap back on. This image looks a lot like number one, doesn't it? Which art words

would you use to describe it? Maybe attic, kylix and tondo? That's right! It's a round (tondo) shallow bowl (kylix) with black-figures on orange clay (attic). You're going to be a pro at this by the time we are done! You can find this kylix — "Theseus and the Minotaur" — at the Louvre in France. The Louvre is world's most-visited museum, with cool paintings like the Mona Lisa and amazing Greek statues. Side note: If you ever head to Paris to see the Louvre, head to the basement! Before it was a fancy museum, the Louvre was a fortress. You can see remnants of the 12th Century fortress down there. You can do a little more research on kylixes on Wiki-media Commons before you go. There are so many cool things to see!

Source: Louvre Museum, Public domain, via Wiki-media Commons

5. This sculpture is a **bust** - a sculpture featuring someone's head, shoulders and chest. I think my bust looks really cool, except for two big problems - my hands are gone! Here's another cool thing about this bust - it's actually a Roman copy of a Greek statue. The Romans loved to copy the Greeks — from their gods to their gardens. The original version of this statue was part of a fountain in Athens. It included Theseus, too. You can find both of our busts, sculpted by Myron, at the National Archeological Museum in Greece. Important note: Theseus' bust is missing half his head. I guess you could say he's feeling a little lightheaded. Ha! Find out more about this photo of my bust by Marsyas at Wikimedia Commons.

Source: Marsyas,   CC   BY-SA   3.0   <http://

creativecommons.org/licenses/by-sa/3.0/>, via Wikimedia Commons

6. A **cartographer** is someone who makes maps. This map of Crete was made by the Dutch cartographer, Dirck Jansz van Santen around 1680. If you head over to the Royal Library of the Netherlands, you can find many maps that Dutch cartographers created during this time period. You can also find out more about these maps (and the copper plates used to make them) at Wikimedia Commons.

Source: Dirck Jansz van Santen, Public domain, via Wikimedia Commons

7. This picture was taken by an astronaut in space! That's right — it's from NASA and the International Space Station. Compare this photo to the hand drawn map. What differences do you see? You can take a look through NASA's other space photos at Nasa.gov.

Source: Nasa, https://images.nasa.gov/details-iss028e018562

8. Amphoras, oh my! Greek pottery is the best. If you head to Greece, you'll find many more amphoras like this one at the National Archaeological Museum in Athens. If you can't get on a plane, you can take a virtual tour of the museum here: https://www.namuseum.gr/en/ or take a deeper look at this amphora at Wikimedia Commons thanks to Codex.

Source: Codex, CC BY-SA 3.0 <https://creativecommons.org/licenses/by-sa/3.0>, via Wikimedia Commons

9. In this photograph by Marc Ryckaert, you can see the ruins of **Gortyna**, a town in Ancient Crete. At this

archaeological site, you'll find columns and archways leading to temples, baths, and theaters. I'm not just talking about baths like the tub in your house. Gortyna had public baths that were larger and much busier! You can find out more about Gortyna and zoom in on this photo at Wikimedia Commons.

Source: Marc Ryckaert (MJJR), CC BY 3.0 <https://creativecommons.org/licenses/by/3.0>, via Wikimedia Commons

10. Photographer Bernard Gagnon captured this photograph of the North Portico of the **Palace at Knossos.** The palace is the setting for my story. The labyrinth wove its way around the grounds, with King Minos ruling over it all. The Palace is a very real location in Crete that was renovated extensively (super fixed up a lot) by archaeologist Sir Arthur Evans. Find out more about the palace at Wikimedia Commons.

Source: Bernard Gagnon, CC BY-SA 3.0 <https://creativecommons.org/licenses/by-sa/3.0>, via Wikimedia Commons

11. Can you believe it? This image is carved into a pendant. You can find it in the British Museum's collection — it's made of gold, enamel, and cornelian (an orange mineral). Sometimes, when we study history, we look at giant palaces and photos from space, and sometimes we look at the smallest gems. Zoom in on this one at Wikimedia Commons.

Source: Nidara, Public domain, via Wikimedia Commons

12. Olaf Bausch took this photo of this engraved tablet. You can find the image on Wikimedia Commons. The

real tablet is at the Archeological Museum of Sitia in Crete. They have an amazing collection of engraved tablets from the archives room of the Palace at Zakros. While they have tablet upon tablet, they are still struggling to decode the language. No one has deciphered Linear A yet! Perhaps you will?

Source: Olaf Tausch, CC BY 3.0 <https://creativecommons.org/licenses/by/3.0>, via Wikimedia Commons

13. Creating a timeline is never a simple thing. You have to decide what events matter to you the most. You know, going back through archaeological history, we are not always sure what the most important moments were. If there are written records, we have a good idea of the moments that mattered. But when we are sifting through the sands of time, we often look for the cataclysms — the natural disasters and history-changing calamities. That's what you see in this timeline that we made especially for this book. But you should check out the *Find Out More* section for more Crete timelines and historical references.

Source: Created using Canva.com

14. This photo is of an **alabastron**, which is like a fancy perfume bottle. This clay piece is at the Archaeological Museum of Herakleion, but was originally found in Kalyvia on the south side of Crete. This piece is from 1350-1300 BCE. If you look at the earlier timeline, you'll see that's around the Mycenaean period. You can find out more about this photo from Zde on Wikimedia Commons.

15. This is a photo of carved stone. You can find the stone at the New Acropolis Museum in Athens. This photo was taken by Tilemahos Efthimiadis. I love this photo because it shows an Ancient Greek explanation of the construction of the statue of **Athena Parthenos**. It was carved by Phidias out of gold and ivory (chryselephantine, to be exact). It's a famous statue, but it's no longer around. My friends said it was about 37 feet tall - that's bigger than me! I wish I could have met that ginormous shining statue, but instead, we'll just have to read about her at the New Acropolis Museum and at Wikimedia Commons.

16. This picture is different from the others! This is an illustration drawn by Monika Hunackova. It is a chalkboard square map of Greece. You can see Crete - the giant island at the bottom. If you love maps, check out the interactive map at Brittanica Kids. It will help you get a sense of where Greece is located (plus, you can Zoom in on Crete!).

17. Wolfgang Sauber snapped this photo of this **Marine Style** (think ocean and waves) flask in the Archaeological Museum in Herakleion. You've heard me mention that Museum before. It holds the largest collection of Minoan artifacts. In fact, it is nearby the Palace at Knossos. You can find the photo at Wikimedia Commons if you can't make it to Crete.

Source: Wolfgang Sauber, Public domain, via Wikimedia Commons

18. This bronze sculpture from Crete is in the British Museum. The photo was taken by Carole Raddato, but the sculpture was made in 1700 - 1450 BCE by...we don't know! We do know that the artisan most likely pounded down sheets of bronze with a hammer to get the shapes they wanted. The bull is significantly larger that the torero - the bull-leaper. That leads historians to believe that the Minoans saw the bull as sacred and important. You can get a close up of this image at Wikimedia Commons.

Source: Carole Raddato from Frankfurt, Germany, CC BY-SA 2.0 <https://creativecommons.org/licenses/by-sa/2.0>, via Wikimedia Commons

19. This sarcophagus was excavated from a tomb in Crete. You can now find it at the Heraklion Archaeological Museum. Scholars were excited to find this fancy coffin because it shows numerous funeral and burial customs in a Minoan/Mycenaean style. The unexpected thing? It also reminds archaeologists of Ancient Egyptian religion. Maybe that is why we were thinking about mummies, eh?

Source: Heraklion Archaeological Museum, CC0, via Wikimedia Commons

20. I made this DOTS image on Canva, and you can make one too! Just go to Canva.com and start creating your own graphics!

Source: Created using Canva.com

21. Does this statue look different to you? It's much younger than many of the artifacts we've seen so far and

has a lot more detail. You can even see Zeus' abs! Wait, is it really Zeus, or is it the Roman god, Jupiter? The Romans pulled many things from the Greeks, from religion to art to architecture. This statue is a Roman copy of a Greek statue made by Pheidias for Zeus' temple at Olympia. The statue was so popular that many artists made imitations and told stories about the statue. The one you're looking at is tall (for a human). It's 6.75 feet tall! You can head to the Getty Villa in California to see the statue, or search their collection online here.

Source: Pheidias, CC0, via the Getty Museum

22. You are looking at Mytikas, the tallest peak of Mount Olympus, in this photo from Stolbovsky. You see, Mount Olympus has many peaks. One is even called Thronos Dios — the Throne of Zeus. I can imagine him seated there, looking down on all his people, watching the world change beneath him. Zoom in on the mountaintops at Wikimedia Commons.

Source: Stolbovsky, CC BY-SA 3.0 <https://creativecommons.org/licenses/by-sa/3.0>, via Wikimedia Commons

23. This is a photo of a silver **didrachm**, which was a kind of coin used in Ancient Greece. This coin was found at the palace at Knossos in Crete. That's me stamped into the silver. This coin was found around 400 BCE, and is now in one of the premier coin collections in the world: the Museum of the Bibliothèque nationale de France in Paris, France. They have so many coins there! I'm proud to be exhibited beside so many detailed coins, medals and gems. Marie-Lan Nguyen took this photo, and you can find the image here at Wikimedia Commons.

24. You can see Cerberus on this **hydria,** which is a kind of Greek pottery from the 7th to 3rd century BCE. Have you noticed that archaeologists love naming different types of pottery like hydria? Just like other artifacts, as scholars find similar pieces of pottery, they label them and categorize them together. That helps them identify themes and trends, and see the larger story. On this hydria, we see the story that the potter wanted to share about Cerberus. He was frightening, wasn't he? With his three heads and snakes sprouting from his neck and paws and nose. He was a powerful guardian of the underworld. You can find this hydria at the Louvre in Paris, France, or in this image taken by Bibi Saint-Pol over at Wikimedia Commons.

25. Temples rose to the sky in Ancient Athens. In some places, the pillars are all that remain. Still, we can see this astounding temple in Athens. It is dedicated to Zeus. The photographer captured the sun hitting the pillars. Oftentimes, one of the best time to take a photo is right before the sun rises or the sun sets, so you can get the light hitting just right! You can find more photos of this temple and other Ancient Greek temples at Wikimedia Commons.

26. In this photograph from Sharon Mollerus, you can see the Parthenon stretching toward the sky. The Parthenon was built on the top of a hill in Athens. The hillside is known as the Acropolis, where you can find the remnants of many other temples. The Parthenon was devoted to Athena. It was built in 447 BCE. It hasn't always looked like the picture, though. It has gone through many renovations over the years, and is currently under construction in 2023!

Source: Sharon Mollerus, CC BY 2.0 <https://creativecommons.org/licenses/by/2.0>, via Wikimedia Commons

27. In this sculpture from 480-460BCE, we see Persephone, seated on her throne. The sculpture was found in **Magna Graecia** - Greater Greece. Magna Graecia is an area of Southern Italy that was settled by the Greeks, or where the Greek culture had a big impact on the civilization. The treasures of Magna Graecia are not small — Greek temples stretch toward the sky in Southern Italy! You can view this statue at the Pergamon Museum in Berlin and online at Wikimedia Commons.

Source: Nemracc, CC BY-SA 3.0 <https://creativecommons.org/licenses/by-sa/3.0>, via Wikimedia Commons

28. In the bottom of this kylix (remember - kylix means shallow bowl), you'll find a painted image of my mother, Pasiphae, and me. This kylix was found in Italy - across the sea from where I was born. The story of my birth spread across the Mediterranean. This kylix now sits in the Museum of the Bibliothèque nationale de

France in Paris. Zoom in on a close-up photo at Wiki-media Commons.

Source: BnF Museum, Public domain, via Wikimedia Commons

29. This is a photo of an illustration that French artist Paul Gustave Louis Christophe Doré did of my stepdad (UGH). Doré drew this illustration for Dante Alighieri's famous poem, *The Inferno*. If you haven't read it, it's about Dante's journey through the Underworld. Along the way, he met Minos and other historical and mythical characters. You can find many of those illustrations at Wiki-media Commons. What's that? This illustration looks like photo number three? VERY ASTUTE! It is from the same series of drawings. Good eye, my friend.

Source: Gustave Dore, Public domain, via Wikimedia Commons

30. This illustration is from H.A. (Hélène Adeline) Guerber's book *The Story of Greeks*. Notice the shading in the illustrations. Pushing a pencil down hard makes the drawing look like it's in the front, while the pencil is lighter in the back, as it climbs toward the sun, making the image fade away. It makes it look like Icarus is close to the sun. Isn't it amazing what we can do with just a pencil and a piece of paper? Look at the story being told. Daedulus does not know that Icarus has fallen. He looks out at us. He is focused on the escape, but we know the rest of the story. See the image and find out more at Wiki-media Commons.

Source: H.A. Guerber, Public domain, via Wikimedia Commons

31. Look familiar? That's right! It's another illustration

from H.A. (Hélène Adeline) Guerber's book *The Story of Greeks*. Notice the shading this time. I'm coming out of that dark entrance. It looks like I'm the bad guy, right? Bonking Theseus with rocks while he holds up his shield in defense? Well, look a little closer at the image. See his sword in the bottom right corner? He is attacking me! This illustration is meant to make me look dangerous. Does it work for you? Take a deeper look at Wikimedia Commons.

Source: H.A. Guerber, Public domain, via Wikimedia Commons

32. I love that the final image of this book is my sister, Ariadne, and her partner, Dionysus. This image is a picture of a piece of sculpted bronze. Over time, it has turned a gorgeous shade of green. When bronze turns green, we say it has a patina. I think a patina is a good way to think about myths and stories: they just get better over time.

Source: British Museum, Public domain, via Wikimedia Commons

10

GLOSSARY

We mentioned a lot of terms, people, and ideas in this book. You can look them up here. Each of these terms is simplified here to make them easier to remember.

Achilles: the prince of Troy and the most famous warrior in the Trojan War, invincible except for his Achilles Heel
Acropolis: a fortress built on a high hill in Athens
Alabastron: a fancy perfume bottle
Amphora: a fancy, decorated storage container
Apollo: the Greek god of the sun
Archaeologist: person who studies ancient civilizations and history through remains and objects left behind
Ariadne: the daughter of Pasiphae and King Minos who eventually married Dionysus and became a goddess
Artifacts: old objects made by humans
Asphodel Meadows: part of the underworld where ordinary people went to live

Asterion: half-man, half-bull, all-awesome son of the Cretan Bull and Pasiphae who dwelled in the labyrinth

Athena Parthenos: a giant statue of Athena

Attic: pottery from Attica, a region in Greece

Audience: the people hearing, watching, and/or reading a story or work of art

Bilingual: in pottery, it means those Ancient Greek paintings and ceramics that use both black and red/orange.

Bust: a sculpture featuring someone's head, shoulders and chest.

Cartographer: a person who makes maps.

Cecrops: the first king of Athens

Cerberus: the hellhound who guarded the gates of hell

Charon: the ferryman who takes you across the river and into the realm of the dead

Citadel: a fancy word for fortress

City-state: a city that had its own laws, army, and coins

Constellations: groups of stars

Course landaise: the French sport of bull-leaping

Crete: the best island in the world, just south of the Greek mainland, home of Asterion the Minotaur

Cretan Bull: sent by Poseidon to King Minos, this majestic snow-white bull was the father of Asterion

Crommyonian Sow: the giant pig-monster that was the child of the monster Echdina and the giant Typhon

Culture: a group of people

Daedulus: the skilled craftsmen and architect that built the labyrinth

Deities: a fancy word for gods

Demeter: the goddess of the harvest

Didrachm: a coin used in Ancient Greece

Dionysus: the god of wine

Elemental: like the weather

Elysian Fields/ Elysium: the part of the underworld where people go after they die if they lived a good life

Evidence: facts, information, or objects that show that something is true

Folklore: the stories, art, and culture people create and pass down

Gortyna: a town in Ancient Crete and a famous archaeological site

Hades: the Lord of the Dead

Hero's Journey: a story pattern often followed in stories about Ancient Greek heroes

Heroine's Journey: a story pattern that is more internal – based on identity instead of quests or an external journey

Hydria: is a kind of Greek pottery from the 7th to 3rd century BCE

Hypothesis: an educated guess

Icarus: son of Daedalus who died when he flew too close to the sun and the wax in his wings melted

Knossos: an archaeology site on Crete, home of King Minos, and the world's oldest city

Kylix: a drinking cup

Labors: important tasks that heroes have to do

Labyrinth: an maze that either has many paths or one long and winding path

Linear A: an early Minoan writing system

Loukoumades: delicious Greek fried donuts

Magna Graecia: an area of Southern Italy that was settled by the Greeks, or where the Greek culture had a big impact

Marine Style: a style of Cretan pottery that includes octopuses and ocean life

Millennia: a period of a thousand years

Minoan: a BCE civilization on Ancient Crete

Minor Gods: gods that are not part of the Olympians, Titans, Primordial Gods, and Nature Gods

Minotaur: See ASTERION

Minos: the son of Zeus and Europa, stepdad to Asterion, and the tyrant king of Crete

Mortals: you humans

Mount Olympus: the highest mountain in Greece and the home of the Olympians

Mycenaean: Ancient Greek civilization that settled on Crete after the Minoans

Myth/Mythology: the beginning stories of a group of people

Nature Gods: gods of the forest, the ocean, the air, and the earth

Odysseus: the famous Greek hero-king who is written about in the ancient epic *the Odyssey*

Olympians: the twelve immortal Greek gods and goddesses who were the sons and daughters of the titans

Palace at Knossos: King Mino's palace, an archaeological site in Crete where the labyrinth once stood

Pantheon: all the Greek gods combined

Parthenon: an Ancient Greek fortress

Pasiphae: the mother of Asterion who was married to King Minos

Peloponnesian War: the war between Athens and Sparta

Persephone: the daughter of Demeter, the goddess of the

harvest, and Zeus, the ruler of the gods, Persphone represents the changing seasons

Poseidon: the god of the sea

Primordial Gods: the first Greek gods of creation who literally formed the heavens and the earth

Rituals: ceremonies dedicated to the gods

Sacred: holy and connected to the gods

Sarcophagus: a fancy coffin that you put in a tomb instead of in the ground

Scientific Method: a process for figuring out what is true using research, testing, and experiments

Setting: the time and place of the story

Sparta: a dominant military power and city-state in Ancient Greeks

Theseus: a prince and later king of Athens, Theseus was a Greek hero and possible son of Poseidon who battled Asterion the Minotaur in the labyrinth

Titans: the sons and daughters of the Primordial Gods

Tondo: a round piece of art

Torero: a bullfighter

Trojan Horse: a Greek wooden horse, given to the Trojans during the Trojan War, that hid Odysseus and his army

Underworld: the Greek world of the dead

Zeus: the ruler of the Greek gods

You made it to the end! Want to read more? We've got you covered. Bring your FIND OUT MORE section to your local library and dive into new worlds of wonder.